With love to
Pastor Michael

With love
[signature]

pastorsamore@gmail.com
240-252-8958

MW00677032

Purpose Redefined

Leveraging Your Core Intelligence for Global Impact

GODKULTURE
PUBLISHING

Sam Ore

This publication may not be reproduced, stored in a retrieval system, or transmitted in whole or in part, in any form or by any means, electronic, mechanical, photocopying, recording, or otherwise, without prior written permission of the publisher. All rights reserved solely by the author. The author guarantees all contents are original and do not infringe upon the legal rights of any other person or work.

Purpose Redefined:

Leveraging Your Core Intelligence for Global Impact

Copyright © 2012 by **Sam Ore**

Paperback ISBN 978-0-9839613-7-6

eBook ISBN 978-0-9839613-8-3

Library of Congress Control Number 2012943554

Published by

GodKulture Publishing

Chicago, Illinois

Phone: 402-419-1072

Email: publishing@GodKulture.org

www.GodKulturepublishing.com

Unless otherwise indicated, all Scripture quotations are taken from the New King James Version of the Holy Bible. Copyright © 1982 by Thomas Nelson, Inc. Used by permission. All rights reserved.

Scripture quotations taken from *The Message*. Copyright © 1993, 1994, 1995, 1996, 2000, 2001, 2002. Used by permission of NavPress Publishing Group.

Printed in United States of America

Dedication

This book is dedicated to:

Everyone who is under pressure because of their multi-giftedness. It was written with you in mind. To the ever faithful leaders and members of Kingdom Ambassadors Christian Center, you are the best people any pastor could have the privilege to lead. Thank you so much.

Debby, my lovely wife: You are the best experience that has happened to me apart from my relationship with Christ. You are a colossal prodigy. Your patience and genuine understanding of my complexities and your willingness to adapt coupled with God's grace have qualified you to lead families to their destinies. I am privileged to be your husband. I love you.

Dunamis: You are our first born, the beginning of our strength, beautiful and intelligent. Your love for the Lord is always demonstrated by the company you keep. This is commendable for a teenage girl in a changing, reckless, morally decadent world. Thank you for allowing me to speak into your destiny. You will lead your generation to the Lord. I love you.

Faith: Your idiosyncrasies and mannerisms remind me of when I was a teenager. You are soon becoming the tallest man in the family. I believe this book will help you focus on your core, God-given gift with which to achieve His purpose on earth. Thank you for allowing me to mentor you and speak into your destiny. I love you.

Nicole: You are daddy's little girl. Always wanting to do a piggy back ride with me. Your love for Jesus Christ is contagious. At eight years old, you are always reminding me to spend more time with my family. I believe you are a great leader destined to fulfill your purpose. I love you.

Casey: Your conception and birth was prophetic. You are the "whiz kid" of the family; the whole world is waiting for your witty inventions that will bless humanity. Thanks for listening to dad when he says, "enough of computer, it's time to go to bed." Boy, I love you.

Acknowledgements

First and foremost, I acknowledge the Almighty God who "anointed my pen to help my generation and the next." These were His words to me many years ago.

I was a hopeless dreg when you picked and cleaned me up. I would serve you in honor and integrity as I focus on your love for me. That way, I could respond to your love in a more efficient way. Thank you, Dad.

To my Lord and Savior, Jesus Christ who paid the supreme price to redeem my soul. When I get to heaven I have only one question for you, "Why did you have to go through all that because of me?" but until then I promise to preach this message of grace that would empower people to be and do what they have been called to do. Thank you Sir.

To the sweet Holy Spirit, my trusted Friend, and Senior partner. Without you, life becomes boring and stressful. Your presence on earth has unleashed an unusual release of God's grace to help humanity. The inspiration and content for this book was orchestrated by your promptings. Thank you for always being there for me.

I would also like to acknowledge the various people who have contributed to my life whether directly or remotely in person or through their resources, especially those who work or gave one way or another to this project. Your labor of love will not go unrewarded. Thank you, Segun Adebayo, Rotimi Kehinde, and the entire team at Godkulture Publishing. You are simply fabulous.

Contents

PART THREE: UNMASKING THE REAL YOU

PART FOUR: ON THE MOVE

PART FIVE: THE APOCALYPSE

Introduction

The time was 11:00 a.m. on that beautiful Friday morning in the hustling and bustling of Reagan National airport in Washington, D.C. The U.S. Airways flight attendant announced my flight to Las Vegas. Looking down below from the window after takeoff as I always do, revealed a clear horizon as a result of the bright summer weather. The journey was smooth. Arriving into Las Vegas airspace and looking through the window, I could see the splendid, sprawling city below that seemed to spread to infinity.

The plane landed without any hassle, thanks to God. I was staring at the magnificent airport and admiring all the beautiful architectural wonders and the different people from all walks of life who were either in Vegas for vacation, business or other endeavors. I was being chauffeured to the famous Caesar's Palace nestled around other hotels in the heart of the city. The glamour was indescribable, the beauty grandiose. I finally checked into my room, but then the unimaginable happened. I plummeted into a deep depression and all my excitements about the trip evaporated into thin air. "What is happening to me?" I asked. After a series of self-evaluation through the help of the Holy Spirit, I knew I was in the wrong place with a good intention (what an oxymoron). I realized that money, fame, and glamour may not necessarily translate into personal fulfillment.

I had come to Las Vegas for an ethical, terrific business meeting that I later realized was not for me. It was supposed to be a three day event. By Sunday morning, my depression climaxed. I knew I was supposed to be behind the pulpit preaching, but here I was in a business presentation. I told God in my hotel room, "If you give me another opportunity, I will return to my base in Maryland to do what you have called me to do with laser focus until I see you face to face." Of course, you should have guessed the outcome of my decisions by now. I pulled out from every business deal that could distract me from my main, core assignment as a minister of the gospel.

However, God began to encourage me. He showed me that my experiences are not necessarily a waste because realistically, millions of people all over the world are currently in my shoes—those who seem to have a Midas touch. Everything they touch becomes gold, but only for a season. Have you met individuals who seem to have diverse abilities to succeed at almost everything? The only problem is that because they spread themselves too thin, they become overloaded, come under pressure, and finally cave in. The results are usually devastating—poverty, sickness, hopelessness, and even in some worst case scenarios, death.

The culprit is not usually the diversity of their gifts, but lack of understanding of what to do with those multiple abilities. What is supposed to be a plus has now become a minus. If this describes you, then you are my target audience. I want to help you because my pain is your gain. I have pragmatically studied God's word, and researched certain strategies that will help you navigate through the stress of multi-giftedness.

The research is a mix of intellectual and spiritual analysis of God's original, unchanging intent for you. The word "purpose," which is one of the most over used words today, has been confused with talents and gifts. Even though in some cases, they can be closely intertwined, the dichotomy is didactically underscored.

You are encouraged through this book to participate intelligently in your own destiny. Enough passivity. Grace should not be confused with inactivity. I am big on God's grace and faith but God's word says *"faith without work is dead"* (James 2:26). In fact, I believe that the true meaning of grace is doing something with the grace you have received.

For instance, it is your responsibility to find out from God what your core, dominant gift in life is, then develop and deploy it. But as simple as that sounds, it is actually the difference between success and failure, riches and poverty, health and sickness, happiness and depression.

Having studied the wealthy and the successful, the concepts discussed in this book from a contemporary and Bible point of view are what make the difference. Unfortunately, only few of these successful people can teach or intelligently transfer what has made them successful to others.

Some of them with good intention mystify it by simply attributing their success to the "grace of God." While that is true, I also believe that the same grace is available to others which makes success in life predictable. Some of the ideas that I conceptualized include the philosophy of creative personal branding, strategic marketing, value added strategic systems, biblical transition strategies, the theory of reverse negatives and how you can leverage your expertise and success into other areas of life where you are equally gifted, which is one of the central messages of this book.

The truth is, successful people have learned to focus on one thing at a time and later leverage their significance into other areas of life. That's exactly what venture capitalists do in the business world. I firmly believe that you are truly successful only when people cannot rationally explain your success based on your effort. In other words, you are so successful, yet in their eyes you are not doing anything. That is when your dreams and the main thing you are born to do juxtapose with what is making you successful. It is like being wealthy for who you are through your God-given gift and the grace of God. Now, that is purpose.

The synergy of pre-redemption gifts and ascension gifts are also concisely explained. Both are going to play major roles in expanding God's Kingdom and bringing in the final harvest as we invade the Kingdoms of this world. You have been pre-ordained by God to take a mountain or Kingdom for Him using your core gift or gifts. Our collective purpose is to displace the callous mafia and the cartels sitting on the thrones of such Kingdoms as:

1.   Political/Governments
2.   Entertainment, sports, arts,
3.   Business/Economy
4.   Religion
5.   Education
6.   Family
7.   Media

This book will show you the strategies we will all employ in these last days to get the job done. At the end of the last chapter, it is my prayer that you will come out with an objective, self-evaluation of your strengths, and what to focus on first before thinking about leveraging your expertise and success in other areas. If you are already successful in your core strengths, isn't it time for you to prayerfully and strategically consider leveraging for a greater impact and significance?

If the seven billion people on the planet know what to do with their lives and how to do it, crime rates will drastically reduce. The real problem in my opinion is not terrorism as horrific as it is (some terrorists actually think they are doing God a service), the real problem is not divorce. People go into marriage because somebody told them a lie that marriage will give them joy, whereas joy can only be found in God's presence. True joy can only be experienced in a marriage where the husband and wife each pursue God's presence and His purpose for their lives.

The real problem is not even lack of purpose for some people but when, where and how they are supposed to get started. My focus is to give you effective, contextual, real life, practical, workable strategies that will empower you to do that purpose no matter where you are in life. It is my belief that my small contribution to the ongoing work of the Holy Spirit in the lives of other leaders around the world will be adequately effective in these last days.

Sam Ore
Silver Spring, Maryland

Part One

THE EPIPHANY

Chapter 1

THE ANATOMY OF PURPOSE

The Four Pillars of Purpose

Have you ever thought that your passion, gifts, talents, and purpose are the same? A lot of people do. In an attempt to define purpose, many complicated synonyms have been used. The only problem with that is, many innocent people trying to pursue their purpose in life have been left between the rock and the hard place.

The challenge becomes more complex with people that have multiple abilities. Unfortunately, many well-meaning, successful leaders have unconsciously given the impression that a successful deployment of one's gift is the same thing as fulfilling purpose. Others believe that being actively involved with some charities is fulfilling purpose. The two propositions are not far from the truth but they are half truth. However, half truth is more dangerous than a complete lie. It is called heresy. Heresy is a combination of truth and lie.

If you are dealing with a blatant, pathological liar with whom you are familiar, you are not likely going to lower your guards, but it becomes more difficult when you are hanging out with someone whose words you cannot consistently trust because he is neither here or there.

The purpose of this book is not to give a thumbs-down on those who have spoken or written on the subject of purpose but to add a new approach to the theme of purpose and perhaps ameliorate certain confusions associated with it.

Without sounding fastidious, I became dissatisfied with the general, perceived definition of purpose and decided to bite the bullet by shedding more light in the dark area of one of the most important words on the planet—PURPOSE.

When God created man, He had a purpose in mind. He designed

every individual in such a way that they can only be fulfilled when they discover and get involved with His purpose for bringing them into this world and start walking in it.

I have read many books on the subject, but the Bible still remains the most authentic, and whatever God says in it is final. Any attempt to distort it leaves the human race more confused. There is a need for us to go back to God in order to understand His purpose for our lives. I have been in such situation of uncertainty before, and I had to go to God to unfold the true meaning of purpose to me.

In my quest, God began to unveil to me concepts that are far beyond what I read from any book. What I am presenting to you in this book is an exciting spiritual odyssey. So, let's take the journey together.

Several people today have read so many books and listened to so many speakers, but sadly enough many have been left more confused. In fact, there are some Christians who are trying to find out what their purpose in life is by listening to speakers who are not even themselves connected to God. So there is a limit to what such speakers who don't have the Spirit of God can offer them. I do not have anything against such people because I am a motivator myself, and more so, every good speaking and teaching has elements of motivation. To motivate means to stir up. You are probably in the wrong vocation if you are preaching and your message is not inspiring.

My focus in this chapter is to do an overhaul of the dichotomy of purpose, gifts, and talents, so that purpose can be clearly understood in the context of God's infallible words.

Every God-given purpose must have some definite features and qualities, four of which are expounded below.

PILLARS OF A GOD-GIVEN PURPOSE

1. **The Universality of Purpose:** Purpose must be universal. In other words, it must align with God's overall purpose and must have the capacity to bless the human race because God's original intention was to rule and govern the earth through humans. Therefore, your life's assignment must be in concordance with

God's original purpose of making the earth a colony of heaven. The book of Genesis states that man was created to govern and subdue the earth.

"(26)Then God said, 'Let Us make man in Our image, according to Our likeness; let them have dominion over the fish of the sea, over the birds of the air, and over

> *If your mission on earth is not in alignment with the general purpose of God, then it is falling short of that particular feature.*

thecattle, over all the earth and over every creeping thing that creeps on the earth.' (27)So God created man in His own image; in the image of God He created him; male and female He created them. (28)Then God blessed them, and God said to them, 'Be fruitful and multiply; fill the earth and subdue it; have dominion over the fish of the sea, over the birds of the air, and over every living thing that moves on the earth.' (29)And God said, 'See, I have given you every herb that yields seed which is on the face of all the earth, and every tree whose fruit yields seed; to you it shall be for food. (30)Also, to every beast of the earth, to every bird of the air, and to everything that creeps on the earth, in which there is life, I have given every green herb for food'; and it was so" (Gen. 1:26-30).

If your mission on earth is not in alignment with the general purpose of God, then it is falling short of that particular feature. Until you start doing what you are wired for, you will not be fulfilled in any undertaking you venture into.

2. **The Immutability of Purpose:** Secondly, every God-given purpose is immutable and irrevocable. In other words, nothing can change it. It is permanent but can have variations or derivatives. For example, if your divine assignment is to be an international evangelist and you backslide and get restored, God is not going to change His mind concerning your original call to be an evangelist because you strayed away; though it could take you more time to finish your journey of purpose. God will restore your wasted years because "the gifts and the calling of God are irrevocable" (Rom.11:29). God's purpose for your life is not a choice but a discovery. His choice for you is always the best and most suitable.

3. **The Profitability of Purpose:** Your divine purpose must add value to humanity. Your purpose is not just about you, but also about others. It must improve the lives of people. A God-given purpose must focus on adding value to people's lives. If it is just all about

you, it is already fraught with deficiencies that have the capacity to be counterproductive. Some of the fundamental questions to always ask yourself when embarking on any endeavor are: how does what I am trying to do benefit other people; how many people will this vision bless; am I just doing this to make profit? If everything starts and ends with you only, then the objective is defective.

4. **Glorifying the Source of Purpose:** Your life's assignment must glorify God because we are created for His pleasure. This, in my opinion, is the most important pillar of any God-given purpose.

"The heaven, even the heavens, are the LORD's; but the earth He has given to the children of men" (Ps. 115:16).

"(9)...Our Father in heaven, Hallowed be Your name. (10)Your kingdom come. Your will be done on earth as it is in heaven" (Matt. 6:9-10).

God wants us to administer this earth on His behalf. Our Creator is the God of the heavens, and it is our responsibility to turn this planet into His colony. We are God's ambassadors on earth and we are to enforce His Kingdom in this earth realm. Some African countries such as Nigeria and Ghana which were once under the British rule, had national, structured life-styles that reflected that of the imperial colonial masters.

For example, in the nineteenth century, left-hand driving was made mandatory in Britain, and such nations which were part of the British Empire followed suit before they became independent. These once colonized nations represented Britain in their own countries. Everything was done to reflect the glory of Britain and that of Her royal majesty. So likewise, we are to conduct our affairs in this world in the heavenly fashion to bring glory to God.

THE DICHOTOMY OF PURPOSE, GIFTS, AND TALENTS

As I mentioned earlier, the expressions of gifts, talents, and abilities have been misconstrued by many to be their life's purpose. That is not entirely true. Several people in the world today, who have made lots of money with their developed gifts and talents, are not satisfied because those divine endowments were channeled incorrectly. Historically, there are two types of gifts or talents. The first one is called the

PRE-ASCENSION GIFTS or PRE-EXISTENCE GIFTS, which simply refer to gifts that were given to you before there was sin. These are gifts or abilities that were packaged in you before you physically existed. The first man, Adam, was so intelligent that he named all the animals which God created, before he fell to the deception of satan because he was made in the image of God. Regardless of the fall of man, all humans, including non-believers, have the innate capability to exhibit their unique skills to profit.

Pre-redemption gifts are abilities that were given to you before you were conceived in your mother's womb. For instance, charisma, the skill of public speaking, has to be operating in the lives of people whom God intended to be in politics or other public related enterprises before they can be established in those vocations, regardless of their religious backgrounds. The following Scriptures attest to the truth of pre-existence gifts.

"(4)Then the word of the LORD came to me, saying: (5)'Before I formed you in the womb I knew you; before you were born I sanctified you; I ordained you a prophet to the nations'" (Jer. 1:4-5).

"(3)Blessed be the God and Father of our Lord Jesus Christ, who has blessed us with every spiritual blessing in the heavenly places in Christ, (4) just as He chose us in Him before the foundation of the world"

(Eph. 1:3-4).

Even before God said *"Let there be light"* (Gen. 1:3), you existed in God. You actually existed before the world began. I strongly believe that Pre-existence gifts are the special abilities demonstrated in politics, sports, education, business, arts, and entertainment. There are many non Christians who do not have a clue about the Holy Ghost and yet are very gifted. Who gave them the gifts? God! James 1:17 says *"Every good gift and every perfect gift is from above..."* They were packaged with those gifts by God before they were born.

He also gave them the free will to use them to expand His Kingdom on earth; the choice is up to them. But we are all responsible for the repercussion of our decisions because all humans will give account of their stewardship of the gifts of God in their lives.

STILL ON PRE-EXISTENCE GIFTS

Let's face it. Do you know of people who are without Christ, and are authorities in their areas of expertise? In fact, the world is being "ruled" by unbelievers because Christians are not manifesting their particular abilities. Majority of the so called freethinkers stand out in their fields of endeavor and have become forces to be reckoned with. For instance, Aristotle and Plato are long dead but people, including believers, still make reference to their ideologies.

A case in point, the concept of "democracy" as a political form of government in which governing power is derived from the people was invented by Greek philosophers who are no longer alive.

The word "democracy" comes from the Greek word *democratia*. The people who originated it are dead but democracy is still thriving all over the world today. Even people in the Middle East are currently staging peaceful demonstrations for democracy. This is why people say that the ideas of men live after them. In the same manner, the music legend Michael Jackson, sold more copies of his songs when he died than when he was alive.

This implies that this talented man made more money in the grave than when he was alive. That is something to think about because some people who are alive are struggling, while a dead man is still making money. Your gifts are the expression of your purpose on earth.

ASCENSION GIFTS are the gifts given to the church, members of the body of Christ, when Jesus rose from the dead and He ascended to heaven.

"(10)He who descended is also the One who ascended far above all the heavens, that He might fill all things. (11)And He Himself gave some to be apostles, some prophets, some evangelists, and some pastors and teachers, (12) for the equipping of the saints for the work of ministry, for the edifying of the body of Christ" (Eph. 4:10-12).

Who ascended on high? Jesus. Did He give gifts to all? No. In other words, everybody is not going to be an apostle, everybody is not going to be a prophet; everybody is not going to be an evangelist, pastor or teacher.

"(28)And God has appointed these in the church: first apostles, second prophets, third teachers, after that miracles, then gifts of healings, helps, administrations, varieties of tongues. (29)Are all apostles? Are all prophets? Are all teachers? Are all workers of miracles?" (1 Cor. 12:28-29).

The Scriptures above show that not everyone will be called into the five-fold ascension, ministry gift. But everybody does have at least a pre-ascension gift or pre-existence gift which God packaged in them, before releasing them into this world. Some can have both, like most Christians do. Such people could be called into one or two of the five-fold ministry: apostles, prophets, evangelists, pastors, and teachers and they also have other "natural" gifts and abilities to perform other responsibilities in life.

There are concerns for people who are multi-gifted and multi-talented because they could live in this world without any significant achievement if they are not properly guided. God has allowed me to go through a lot of painful experiences so as to be able to help such people. If you are multitalented, congrats! But if you are not taught the skills and the strategies to handle those abilities, they will be counterproductive.

You've got to sit down and evaluate your life, so you don't go round in circle forever. Praise God, I have the answers to your dilemma, from God's word. Are you trying to figure out what you should be doing with your life? You don't have to jump all over the place trying to figure out what to do with your giftings and talents. Confused people frequently enter into certain careers or businesses that seem promising. Such people find it difficult to make headway in life because of their inability to have a purposeful direction and thus will be subjected to other people's whims. They look for immediate gratification and are known as a jack of all trades.

They are not experts in anything. Making money is the motive behind any venture they embark on. On the contrary, they are supposed to be involved in endeavors that will bless the human race, so that through it, money will come to them instead of them chasing after money. In the next chapter, you will learn the specific differences between purpose and gift.

Study Guide

1. Identify three natural gifts you think you could use to make the world a better place.

2. Do you think you do have ascension gifts? If yes, what are they? Apostle __, Prophet __, Evangelist __, Pastor __, Teacher _

3. Do you think you have a combination of both types of gifts? If yes:

   what are they?
   a.
   b.
   c.
   d.

4. Have you been using any of them? If yes, in what capacity? Suggest three action steps that could make you more effective in them.

5. If the answer is no, what are the limitations? Identify the three major ones.
   a.
   b.
   c.

6. Write the proposed remedies with a twenty-one day action plan to address those limitations.
   a.
   b.

7. Identify three trusted, faithful accountability partners for support.
   a.
   b.
   c.

Chapter 2

GIFT VERSUS PURPOSE

The Dichotomy I

It is very crucial to understand the difference between purpose and gifts. For the most part, people use these elements interchangeably as if they are fundamentally the same. They may be closely interrelated but may not be exactly the same. For example, singing could be a gift but may not necessarily fulfill purpose (remember the four elements of purpose in Chapter 1?). For some, purpose and gifting are the same, although it does not necessarily have to be like that for everybody. When some people are asked what their purpose is, they respond by telling you their gifts or passion.

> *Your divine purpose is the reason for your existence, while gifts, abilities, and talents provide a natural habitat or a platform of expression for that purpose.*

In most cases your gifts or talents are basically the expression of your purpose.

A proper understanding of this concept is very imperative. Your divine purpose is the reason for your existence, while gifts, abilities, and talents provide a natural habitat or a platform of expression for that purpose. Purpose has to be discovered and distinct before your talent and gifting can be applied to it for its enrichment. Jesus said:

> *"(18)The Spirit of the LORD is upon Me, because He has anointed Me to preach the gospel to the poor; He has sent Me to heal the brokenhearted, to proclaim liberty to the captives and recovery of sight to the blind, to set at liberty those who are oppressed; (19)To proclaim the acceptable year of the LORD"* (Luke 4:18-19).

The platform or expression of His purpose is the anointing or the gift on His life to preach the gospel to the poor and set the captives free. The anointing was not His purpose, but His purpose was to establish God's kingdom on the earth according to Matthew 6:9-10 where He taught His disciples how to pray.

"⁽⁹⁾In this manner, therefore, pray: Our Father in heaven, Hallowed be Your name. ⁽¹⁰⁾Your kingdom come. Your will be done on earth as it is in heaven" (Matt. 6:9-10).

What is the will of the Father, you may ask? Jesus mentioned several times in the Gospels that His food was to do the will of the Father, which implies that Jesus got involved with the purpose of the Father for Him. He needed the charisma and the gifts for the expression of that purpose. So God had to anoint Him with the gifts of healing so that people could be delivered from their oppressions. Acts 10:38 explains it further.

"How God anointed Jesus of Nazareth with the Holy Spirit and with power, who went about doing good and healing all who were oppressed by the devil, for God was with Him" (Acts 10:38).

He was establishing the reign of God (Kingdom of God) everywhere He went.

Everything Jesus did with His anointing/gifts, and abilities was to establish God's purpose, and Jesus' purpose fits into the four elements of a God-given purpose.

A man can be gifted and greatly talented, but may not fulfill his purpose. So, your abilities and charisma are the catalysts necessary for the manifestation of your purpose. The purpose of a fish is to glorify God while swimming, the gift is the ability to swim. The platform or the natural habitat for the fish to accomplish its reason for existence is water. In the same vein, the primary purpose of a bird is to glorify God while flying, the gift is the ability to fly and the platform to make that possible is the sky. Without the sky, and the gift of flying, the bird will not fulfill its purpose. Without water and the gift of swimming, the fish will not fulfill its purpose. So without the gift and anointing of God, you will not be able to fulfill your God-given purpose of having dominion on earth. You are not supposed to struggle in your life mission on earth if you have the platform or the natural habitat and the gifts to fulfill it. Fish don't enroll in swimming lessons to be proficient in swimming, and neither do birds need to enroll in a flight school. The need to get trained and acquire skills in your divine assignment is all part of the consequences of the fall of man. Originally, it was not so.

Even though these creatures do not enlist for formal training to exhibit their prowess, no human can boast of being a better swimmer than a fish or a better flyer than a bird. As these creatures function conveniently and perfectly in the way God designed them, you are also supposed to fit in naturally in your God ordained purpose through your gifts and abilities.

Struggling to thrive in any vocation could be an indication that you may not be divinely designed for it. Several people wake up in the morning; Monday to Friday, go to jobs they hate simply to pay their bills. You do not exist to pay bills; your existence on earth is more worthwhile than that. There is more to life, God wants you to live everyday with high energy and excitement.

What is the purpose of a star? Its purpose is to glorify God while shinning, the ability to shine is the gift and the natural habitat for that to happen is the firmament. The purpose of the grass or the flower is to glorify God while blooming, the ability to bloom is the gift. Whenever you see a flower, you move closer to it to appreciate its beauty and smell its fragrance. Notice that the fish, the birds, the elements, the grass, and the flowers, apart from glorifying God also fit into the other four elements or characteristics of a God-given purpose. Their operations and functions have never changed, they add values to humanity and they align with God's original intent for man to govern the earth.

Your purpose is to make this world a better place. How do you achieve that? By applying the principles of God as it was in heaven on earth, so that this earth can be turned into heaven's colony.

EFFECTIVE STEWARDSHIP

You can only make this world a better place when you use your gift to advance God's program on earth while fulfilling your purpose. If this is the scenario, you start living and not just existing. In life, the only way to experience joy consistently and the peace of God which surpasses all understanding is when you start using your gifts to enhance God's assignment for you.

Using your divine endowments could give you temporary satisfaction, but in the end will lead to frustration and despondency if they are not changing lives positively. Some talented singers for instance, discovered their gifts while serving in the church, but because of the love of money, they have fully embraced the worldly appeal and are negatively impacting their fans with their songs. There have been cases of people getting high on crack or getting involved in certain sexual perversions as a result of negative influence of certain types of music on them. So, they can't possibly say that singing is their purpose. That would just be a gift because God's purpose is not destructive.

This is a tragedy because they were created by God to be an instrument of deliverance, but are now being used by the devil as tools of destruction. How could they possibly be blamed for the atrocities being perpetrated by their fans you may ask? The truth is, famous people, regardless of their character, are always influencing people especially young ones who look unto them as role models and are sometimes shaped by their opinions. A lot of folks in the entertainment industry are committing suicide because of lack of inner fulfillment. They are famous, charismatic, and have become wealthy in the process of using their talents and giftings. Yet, because they are not fulfilling their divine purpose, they become depressed and some cut their lives short. Remember Club 27? (The young, rising celebrity singers seem to be dying at age twenty-seven).

Fulfillment of God's purpose for man is the only source of ultimate joy in this world, but a person can fulfill certain elements of his or her purpose on earth and still end up in hell if he or she dies in sin.

Ironically, some of the greatest givers and charitable organizations that are making this world a better place are not necessarily followers of Christ in the real sense of it. Regardless of their little or no knowledge of God, they "promote" God's agenda with their giving. In fact, some Christians have to be taught repeatedly before they give out of their material possessions. Most unbelievers don't need that, they just give.

They give to establish schools in poor nations of the earth, support victims of natural disasters, and also bolster charitable deeds around the world. They are using their pre-existence gifts as it were to boost God's agenda in this earthly realm. For instance, Oprah Winfrey has given more than can be expected of any woman.

I don't know of any woman who has given more to noble causes than Ms. Winfrey. Some children would never have imagined being in a good school if not for her kind gesture. She uses her gift of communication for talk shows to showcase and market her abilities. Fulfilling your divine purpose, displaying your gifts, and being born again are three different things people are confused about. You can be temporarily happy when you exhibit your gift, but failure to use it for your God-given purpose can only lead to sadness. Charisma and abilities can make you rich, famous, and happy, but it cannot guarantee a lasting joy because joy can only come from the presence of God.

> *Fulfilling your divine purpose, displaying your gifts, and being born again are three different things people are confused about. You can be temporarily happy when you exhibit your gift, but failure to use it for your God-given purpose can only lead to sadness.*

"For the kingdom of God is not eating and drinking, but righteousness and peace and joy in the Holy Spirit" (Rom. 14:17).

"You will show me the path of life; in Your presence is fullness of joy; at Your right hand are pleasures forevermore" (Ps. 16:11).

Also, a man can be very joyful because he is born again, and filled with the Holy Ghost, but without discovering his gift with which to fulfill purpose, he will be broke, and disgusted. He will speak in tongues but die in poverty and go to heaven. However, a man can have the best of both worlds. He can be born again, discover his purpose, have the fullness of God's grace on the earth, fulfill his purpose and have a lot of good things of this world to show for it. This is because when you begin to fulfill your purpose, success, and everything it represents, will almost automatically gravitate towards you.

In fact, my postulation after researching God's word and studying contemporary events is that there are seven categories and groups of people currently living on the earth. They are effectively analyzed in the Apocalypse, at the end of the book.

Study Guide

---

1. Write down five main things that you are presently struggling with in reference to your gifts and purpose.

    a.

    b.

    c.

    d.

    e.

2. Discuss the following elements. Gifts are:
    a. Expressions of purpose.
    b. Platform for the expression of purpose.
    c. Natural habitat for the expression of purpose.

3. What is the difference between happiness and joy? Give two examples:

    a.

    b.

4. Is it possible for a non-believer to achieve certain elements of God's purpose? If you answer yes, identify those elements with real life examples.

    a.

    b.

5. Write down five strategic action plans you have identified to combat the five challenges in (1) above. Remember to discuss them with your accountability partners.

    a.

    b.

    c.

    d.

    e.

Chapter 3

PASSION VERSUS PURPOSE

The Dichotomy II

As an illustration, if you plan a trip to Vancouver in Canada, and scheduled to leave by 3:00 p.m., by chance you meet an old friend at the airport who is traveling to Frankfurt, Germany and his flight is scheduled for 2:00 p.m. Although he is your pal, you won't want to engage in lengthy discussion with him or her because one or both of you might miss your flight.

In life, I have come to the realization that a lot of people have lost focus of their destiny or purpose because they are hanging out with the wrong crowd. Your life is a bundle of different levels of grace. The whole world wants to hear about what the Creator has exclusively bestowed upon you. He is the only One who deserves the best of your time.

CREATOR'S MANUAL

"[13] The LORD looks from heaven; He sees all the sons of men. [14] From the place of His dwelling He looks on all the inhabitants of the earth;

[15] He fashions their hearts individually; He considers all their works" (Ps. 33:13-15).

The Heavenly Father, Creator and Manufacturer of your life, knows you more than you think you do. He formed your inner most being and knit you together in your mother's womb to perform a unique role on this planet earth. Not only did He wonderfully create you, He also watches over everything you do so that you can be on track with His program for your life. He is the best Person to have engaging discussion with where your gifts and purpose are concerned.

So take time to seek after Him more than you have ever done before because in so doing, you will discover yourself. Everything God has infused in you to bless humanity must be deployed. People are waiting to read your revolutionary poems, books, and to listen to your uncommon music. If your Maker wired you for business, then make an effort to have a profound understanding of business organizations and management dynamics so that yours can stand out in the crowded marketplace. Marketplace in this context is where values are exchanged for money.

This is how your business can thrive and contribute positively to the global economy. Your mission on earth is bigger than you and if you have been reaching out to a small community of people, strive to rediscover your life's purpose in order to broaden your spectrum of influence by fellowshipping with your Maker because He has your life's manual at His disposal. As a result of passive, complacent attitude to life, many people are not optimally applying their gifts and talents to accomplish God's purpose for their lives. It is one thing to discover God's glorious purpose for you, but another thing is to regularly fellowship with Him to know the necessary information on how to better appropriate your abilities as you move from one phase to another in quest of your destiny. This is necessary because God wants you to be a good steward of His diverse grace in your life. If you are not born again, surrender your life to the Lord Jesus and be saved. Ask the Holy Spirit to come upon you so that the eyes of your understanding will be enlightened as you study God's word.

Intimacy with God through a diligent study of His word and worship will unfold His many-sided wisdom that will reveal your personal life to you. As you know yourself better, confusion ceases to exist in your life and you will know exactly what to do on earth and also how to best use your gifts so that they are not redundant.

A lot of people consult with psychics to find out who they are, but those "consultants" themselves need help because they have complex issues in their lives which only God can resolve. So why don't you go back directly to God who can reveal your life to you. Nobody knows a product better than the manufacturer, says Myles Munroe. In order for you to clearly understand your unique purpose, and the relevant core gift needed to pursue it, you need sound clarity which only comes through the process of renewing your mind.

"[1]I beseech you therefore, brethren, by the mercies of God, that you present your bodies a living sacrifice, holy, acceptable to God, which is your reasonable service. [2]And do not be conformed to this world, but be transformed by the renewing of your mind, that you may prove what is that good and acceptable and perfect will of God" (Rom. 12:1-2).

Man is nothing without God and to change from that state of nothingness to the status of making impact, transformation is needed.

The word "transform" comes from the Greek word *metamorphoo*. It is made up of two words; *meta* which means change, and *morphoo* which means form. In the realm of science, it describes the process through which a caterpillar completes its phenomenal makeover into a beautifully mature adult butterfly. Transformation is a gradual process and nobody goes through a complete transformation in one day.

When you pray and study God's word, you are subjecting yourself to be transformed by the Holy Spirit. In that process, your mind is renewed without exerting effort, and consequently God's purpose for your life becomes clearer. The height of this transformational course is called sanctification, which is the process of becoming one with God. This is only made possible by the Holy Spirit through the truths of God's word.

"Sanctify them by your word. Your word is truth" (John 17:17). This is a daily spiritual process God expects you to engage in because in such state, it will not be difficult to discover and walk in your purpose through your gift.

Constant studying of God's word, praying in the Holy Ghost, and fasting are the spiritual exercises you need to do so as to be in tune with God who will reveal to you your divine mission on earth. God wired your heart in such a way, so that through it, you can be led by the Spirit. Therefore, it is imperative not to ignore the promptings of your heart but guard it carefully because out of it flows information about your purpose and destiny. You can be misled by relying on your mind, especially when it is not renewed.

You hear the voice of God clearly in your heart, while renewing your mind with His word. So, do not disregard your inner signals because people achieve greatness when they act from their heart and their passion. Those who learn to recognize the promptings of their heart, and then find the courage to follow them, are the ones who win races, rule nations, and create masterpieces.

They also, regardless of their circumstances, live with a sense of contentment knowing that they are who they want to be.

PASSION VERSUS PURPOSE

Some are confounded that they cannot distinguish between their passion and purpose. Passion is a powerful or compelling emotion or feeling towards something. Your passion does not necessarily stand for your God-given purpose, but it could guide you into it. Care must be taken not to use the word passion interchangeably with purpose. This is because it is possible to be passionate about things that are completely irrele va nt to one's destiny. When your gifts and talents align with your divine mission on earth, then you are on course to fulfilling it.

> *… it is possible to be passionate about things that are completely irrelevant to one's destiny. When your gifts and talents align with your divine mission on earth, then you are on course to fulfilling it.*

For those who are not too spiritual, who find it difficult to pray or fast as they ought to, there is a way that God has designed for them too, in the journey to the discovery of their core gift and life purpose. Numerous people are perplexed and on the verge of giving up in life because of frustration associated with inability to experience their purpose after several years of fasting and prayer. In addition to praying and fasting, there are other ways of knowing your calling and identifying your gifts in life. This is explained into details in another chapter. Selfless living with a good conscience before God can also show the way to your life assignment because God fashioned your heart to be closely connected with Him so as to guide you in the path of life.

Every man born into this world is created in the image of God and there is at least one divine endowment in each person, but it is the duty of each one to recognize and nurture it. God's purpose for Joseph was to govern and rule. The dream of greatness he had when he was young did not come into fruition until he applied his gift of interpretation of dreams.

He was so passionate about his gift that he could not wait to attend to other people having problems with their dreams. His dreams got him into pit and later on, his master promoted him because of his governing skills and integrity. While in prison, he was not depressed, but was again concerned with how to help people with his gifts.

This passion of interpreting dreams led him to the butler and baker in the prison. Two years after interpreting their dreams, Joseph's developed gift made a way for him with Pharaoh, the ruler of the most powerful country on earth at the time. Also, his excellent, governing skills opened the door for a permanent job for him at the palace and consequently, became very influential in the land of Egypt.

"A man's gift makes room for him, and brings him before great men" (Prov. 18:16).

"Do you see a man diligent and skillful in his business? He will stand before kings; he will not stand before obscure men" (Prov. 22:29).

The life of Joseph and the Scriptures above show how a discovered gift can lead to the fulfillment of destiny. After the discovery, it is your responsibility to develop it for the purpose of blessing humanity. Your gift makes room for you as you become an expert in your specialty, and furthermore, life rewards those who nurture and appropriately deploy their abilities.

You become relevant when your dominant gifts and talents line up with your divine purpose. Doing the right things in the right way at the right time makes you outstanding like Joseph. A person cannot amount to anything substantial in this world if he focuses solely on his personal needs. While fulfilling your assignment on earth, your passion, triggered in the right direction towards God's purpose for your life will lead you to mind other people's business so that you can help them out.

The question you should always ask yourself is; what can I do with my gifts and talents that will trigger my divine purpose? The journey to fulfillment begins when you start pondering in your heart how your abilities align with your earthly mission. This gives you the energy to tackle everyday challenges and go for what motivates you because there is a force of purpose driving you.

Some appear not to be passionate about anything because they have not been able to tap into the divine endowment that will arouse their passion. Some appear quiet until you discuss their interest in certain fields, then all their faculties will be awakened because they are passionate about the subject. For example, those who love soccer could lecture you in the history of soccer regarding the country that won the world cup tournament in a particular year, the center referee and the other officials, the colors of the jersey of the two teams that played in the finals, where it was played and other minute details of the event. Also, some people cannot wait till you start talking about computers and you start hearing words like gigabytes, RAM size and so on because their passion is stirred up.

What are you enthusiastic about? What was your recurrent and innocent childhood dream? The words recurrent and innocent are relevant because children can be indecisive and say things with the honesty of their hearts. When you ask a child what he will like to become in life, he could respond with words like "fire fighter, police officer, or pilot."

If you ask him the same question a week later, he may decide to be a teacher. Subsequently, he might change his mind several times to go for other professions. In my childhood days, I planned to join the military because I believed it was a very popular profession and in view of that, promised to buy a car for my mom when I returned from the war front. Later, I discovered that I hated injustice because of the way the class president of my high school abused his authority over his classmates. He acted like a dictator because he had the power to checkmate anyone who misbehaved. I overthrew him so that I could enforce fairness in the system. It was then I found out that part of my destiny was to fight for the right of the oppressed. If you critically examine your collection of childhood memories, you'll begin to discover the pattern of your mission here on earth. What are you willing to commit to, to the point of death? What stirs up your passion? Are you living or just existing?

If you are not ready to go all the way for your divine assignment on earth, you are not ready to live. Paul said in the epistle, *"For to me, to live is Christ, and to die is gain"* (Philippians 1:21). Paul was passionate and very bold to talk about his calling before people in authority at the expense of anything on earth because he knew that either way, whether alive or dead, he was not going to lose anything.

He was able to go through all the challenges in the course of fulfilling his purpose and at the end, boldly declared that he had finished his mission on earth.

"I have fought the good fight, I have finished the course, I have kept the faith" (2 Tim. 4:7).

Notice that His passion was activated in the direction of His purpose. Watch whatever you are passionate about. A positive passion towards a vision that is in consonance with God's agenda may be a clue to your purpose.

Paul discovered his divine purpose when he encountered Jesus on the way to Damascus even though he went through rough-and-tumble in the process of fulfilling his destiny. Before he left this world, he finished his course and I am sure that he must have been given a glorious welcome when he got to heaven because he completed his earthly assignment. The choice is yours whether to keep running the rat race or to effectively put to use your unique abilities to fulfill your purpose.

In this world, you may be given many awards and may be outstandingly celebrated for your magnificent achievements, but to God what is left undone in His purpose for you is much more important. There is no valid benchmark to measure ourselves with as we go about fulfilling our assignment on earth. Only God knows who is great in the final analysis. For instance, if God assigns you a particular task because of your divine makeup and gifts, and you only complete 50 percent of it, the world may praise you because of their myopic perspective in assessing your uncommon abilities. However, to God's standard, you did not complete what He intended for you. By God's grace, by the time I am leaving this world, I want to boldly proclaim that I have finished my divine mission.

Although there may be no legitimate standard on earth to monitor your progress in the journey of destiny, as a Christian you have the Holy Spirit inside of you to guide you in every phase of your earthly assignment. Therefore, endeavor to develop an intimate relationship with Him so that He can keep you on track in your pursuit of purpose.

Always obey His voice and ask Him for clarifications if you are stuck on what to do. If God wants you to write one hundred books and you write fifty, to the people around you, you have done a good job, but to God who has wired you for this responsibility, you only deserve half of the rewards because of your incomplete work.

Some say the cemetery is the wealthiest place in the world because a lot of people who end up there did not discover their purpose and some of those who did were not able to fully release the gifts of God in them to complete their divine mission. My opinion is that the wealthiest resources on earth may be the ones trapped inside the seven billion people currently living. Our concern therefore should not be for the wasted resources in the graves, because they are gone, but for the living who do not know what to do with their lives.

Observe the patterns in your life right from your childhood and you will know what you love to do naturally, which can also lead you to the big picture of your life. It is high time you stopped going to a job you don't like. Many are bound to their job because of the fear of not meeting their financial needs. You can't continue to play safe, so wake up from your slumber and go all the way to pursue your dreams.

In the process, you might experience some setbacks, but if you hold on to what your Maker has revealed to you, there will always be a way out for you. It will not just be a way out for you to survive, but for you to be a blessing to your world and generations yet unborn. Navigating through much confusion associated with passion, gifts, unique talents, and abilities is vividly discussed in another chapter.

Study Guide

---

1. How serious are you in coming to a place of absolute rest as far as your core gift is concerned?
   a. Very serious _____
   b. Serious _____
   c. Indifferent _____

2. On a scale of 1-10, what is your passion level about life in general?

   1   2   3   4   5   6   7   8   9   10

3. Identify three recurrent childhood dreams that have not left you in their order of priority.
   a.
   b.
   c.

4. Have those childhood dreams been manifesting in different forms in your adult life of late? If yes, how? Explain.

5. What is your best learning method? (Books, CDs, DVDs, seminars, etc.) How often do you invest in any of these materials?
   Aggressively _____   Casually _____
   You prefer to borrow learning materials _____

6. If you had a chance between taking care of your hair or buying a resourceful material that is relevant to your gift and purpose in life, which would be more important to you? Explain the reason for your choice below.

7. How many books on your gift have you studied this year?

Chapter 4

FOUR STAGES OF COMPETENCE

Your Life Assignment versus Your Career

Several years ago, psychologists came up with the concept of the four stages of the human developments which illustrate different levels of proficiency. The results of the study conducted show that human beings go through four different stages of growth. Its origin and development is still unknown. Some scholars believe the theory was created and developed at the Gordon Training Institute while some argue that it was developed by Abraham Maslow, an American professor of psychology at Brandeis, Columbia and Cornell Universities.

The academic basis of this theory simply states that there are four stages for learning or acquiring new skills. They are:

1. Unconscious Incompetence
2. Conscious Incompetence
3. Conscious Competence
4. Unconscious Competence

Four Stages of Competence
Table 1

Unconscious Incompetence	A stage where every human neither understands nor knows how to effectively do something, nor recognizes the shortfall, nor has a desire to address it. This could also be the complete child-hood, innocent stage of development.

Conscious Incompetence	A stage when people neither understand nor know how to do something, but they might realize the shortcoming without being able to make up for it. For example, you might be given a car to drive but you are not competent to drive it. You have progressed from the first stage because at least, you are conscious of your inability.
Conscious Competence	This is the stage when a person understands how to do something. However, demonstrating the skill or knowledge requires a great deal of consciousness or concentration. For instance, you may be a good speaker but you need to consciously practice to perfect the skill.
Unconscious Competence	The final stage is when you have practiced a particular skill so much that it has become second nature and can be performed easily without too much attention to it. For instance, you could drive to your workplace every single day while engrossed in a phone conversation with either a friend or spouse without consciously noticing the road and traffic signs and still not miss your way or get involved in accident (that is not advisable though). Other skills that people have developed to a point of unconscious competence include cooking, speaking, reading, singing, writing, mastery of different sports etc. This is the stage where you and the expression of your core gift cannot be separated. It is the level where you become one with your main intelligence after years of consistent faithfulness.

This study is scientific and scriptural. Everybody could relate and experiment with it in almost every endeavor.

The last stage (Unconscious Competence) is the best place to be with reference to your skills and purpose in life; a place where the use of your gifts and the fulfillment of your destiny have become second nature.

Being unconsciously competent in your divine purpose shows you have developed and mastered your personal brand to a point that success comes to you naturally. Your vision and goals in life should be part of your daily experiences that come out of you extemporaneously. For instance, if you are given an opportunity to discuss with the President of the United States for two minutes, what do you intend to say if he graciously asks you to request for anything you want? Some will probably need two hours or more to prepare because they don't know precisely what to tell the most influential man in the world. This could be an indication of a goalless life. Think about it! In 2 Kings Chapter 2, how much time was at Elisha's disposal when Elijah asked him what he wanted before he was taken into heaven? Elisha did not take time out to think or pray about it. In a split second, he asked for the double portion of his master's spirit and consequently got the whole package.

Many people today will probably ask for the bank account of the man of God or his houses. The man knew what he wanted even when there were discouragements, crises, and all kinds of persecutions from the other sons of the prophet who had lost focus in life. Elisha still maintained focus in spite of all the challenges.

BIBLE HEROES OF THE FAITH WHO OPERATED WITH UNCONSCIOUS COMPETENCE

1. Jacob: He so much developed his God-given, unique ability of creative thinking to a point of absolute second nature.

2. Joseph: His precise, relevant dreams and ability to interpret dreams for other people could only come from the realm of unconscious competence.

3. Daniel: In addition to his almost impeccable ability to interpret dreams, his exquisite display of excellent spirit could only emanate from the supernatural realm of unconscious competence.

4. Solomon: The greatest King that had ever lived before Jesus functioned with such flawless wisdom that attracted other royalties from different nations of the earth. Operating at that consistent level of international, royal consulting was not accidental. Such accuracy and consistency of problem-solving advice could only come from somebody whose core gift has become second nature.

5. All the Apostles in the New Testament: Peter, Paul, John, Luke, and the rest of them are also classical examples of people who excelled effortlessly.

6. Jesus Christ: Being the human epitome of the God head, He consistently functioned at the level of infallible grace in every phase of His earthly ministry. Most of the physical miracles He performed were repeated many times including raising the dead.

The reality is, when a man's core gift is identified, developed, and deployed to a point of unconscious competence, the practical results he experiences in his journey of purpose are consistently predictable. When Billy Graham finishes his sermons and the choir sings "Just As I Am," you can predict what follows. Souls would flood the platform. This is because Evangelist Graham has done the same thing for almost six decades. You too should endeavor to take your core gift or main intelligence to this level.

GOD-GIVEN VISION VERSUS CAREER

"You will never make a living with your certificate..." was the statement that reverberated from God to me in 1990. I had gone to a place called "Zion" to have a private fellowship with God in prayer. It was a starry, beautiful night on the University campus where I was a second-year student. The secluded part of the campus very close to the soccer field was designated as Zion where Christians who wanted to go extra miles with God could pray in the night for as long as they wanted.

I had gone there many times, but this particular night will be a destiny molding one.

My ambition was to finish my degree two years later, take one or two advanced professional courses in journalism and become the foremost journalist and publisher in the world. I even promised God to be a "sponsor" of His Kingdom with the money I would make from my career. I later realized I was too small to sponsor God's Kingdom. He doesn't need sponsors; He only needs partners who will consider themselves privileged.

These words are still fresh and are alive till today. They were the beginnings of several, divine encounters God would have with me regarding my purpose in life. "I will take care of you" He concluded after a few hours of fellowship that night. Those words have turned me, a former struggling, confused alcoholic to an amazing story of God's grace influencing people positively on a global scale. I am still waiting for the manifestations of other things from those encounters. Interestingly, because God's words will never fall to the ground, I have never needed to use my certificate to make a living and never will. Now I understand why He allowed me to get the degree. Everything is going full circle. I have written this story to insist that every material blessing, joy, happiness is wrapped up in your core gift and purpose in life. Everything you need is in your gift.

(By the way, please if you are a student, don't pull out of school. By God's grace, in spite of that divine encounter, I still completed my degree and graduated as one of the best students in my entire faculty.)

When you know what to do with your life, it does not necessarily mean that the journey will be smooth sailing. By faith, you have the assurance that in the face of adversities, you are still on course as you focus on your divine purpose because your Maker is there with you every step of the way to see you through to the end of your journey.

You've got to set your face like a flint and be like Paul when he courageously declared;

"(12)Not that I have already attained, or am already perfected; but I press on, that I may lay hold of that for which Christ Jesus has also laid hold of me. (13)Brethren, I do not count myself to have apprehended; but one thing I do, forgetting those things which are behind and reaching forward to those things which are ahead, (14)I press toward the goal for the prize of the upward call of God in Christ Jesus" (Phil. 3:12-14).

It must be understood that your job is not your destiny if it does not give you the ultimate satisfaction or fulfillment that you desire. The job is just a stepping stone for you to discover your divine work. There is a difference between your job and your work. Your work is what you were created to do, which is your life's core gift. You can be relieved of your job if your employer finds someone who can perform your role for less money.

It must be understood that your job is not your destiny if it does not give you the ultimate satisfaction or fulfillment that you desire. The job is just a stepping stone for you to discover your divine work. There is a difference between your job and your work. Your work is what you were created to do, which is your life's core gift.

At the beginning of the information technolog y boom, an average person was making $110,000 a year, but there were also some people who were ready to accept $60,000 per year for the same job. Many people lost their jobs in the process because many companies opted for the folks accepting lower salaries so that they could signif icantly maximize their profits.

No one can fire you from your work (core gift) because your work is your life. Your work is your destiny; your work could also be your purpose. You can be retired from your job or you can resign from it at your own discretion, but you cannot retire from your work because you cannot retire from being yourself. You cannot retire from public speaking if it is your dominant talent because it becomes better as you grow with age.

As far as your job is concerned, your employer runs your life. That may be the bitter truth. Check this out. Your employer tells you when to wake up in the morning. Sometimes, he tells you when to eat breakfast and lunch. He determines when to go on vacation. Worst still, he tells you when to go to church to serve. He is basically in control, except your job is your calling; every job should be a transitional journey to your destiny.

You too at some point can flip the coin and transition into the better side of the equation by becoming the employer. That is the beauty of capitalism and free enterprise. Whoever is brave enough to take the risk will eventually take charge of his destiny. Capitalism rewards innovations and creativity. The fundamental difference between communism and free enterprise is, the former is built on the ideology of "change the environment and the man would change" while the latter is the opposite, "change the man and he will change the environment." No wonder America is called the land of the free and the home of the brave. If you are timid and passive, you will only get handouts. If you are bold and creative and you have intestinal fortitude, coupled with the grace of God, you'll strike gold. Bingo.

THE PHILOSOPHY OF "FULL-TIME WORK"

Have you ever heard people use the term "full-time job" or "full-time profession" before? More often than not, when this expression is used, the assumed, general meaning is that whoever is being referred to is engaged in a certain endeavor that is taking his entire time or attention. The term is popular with preachers, housewives, and even professionals in several fields.

The only unfortunate thing is that while there is nothing wrong with the word itself, the context has been grossly and sincerely misunderstood. If full-time is only used to describe what is taking the best of your time and attention, then you are wrong. However, if it is used to refer to what you have been called to do (your core life assignment) then you are right.

> *The fundamental difference between communism and free enterprise is, the former is built on the ideology of "change the environment and the man would change" while the latter is the opposite, "change the man and he will change the environment."*

The taxonomy is very imperative in the sense that everybody's work (gift and purpose), not job, should be his or her full-time endeavor because it should take you a lifetime to complete it.

So, whatever you are doing now for the primary reason of paying your bills is supposed to be your part-time job. Your calling and your main God-given intelligence or gift is your full-time work. It doesn't have to be "spiritual," it could be as simple as having your own clinic as a doctor or running a restaurant as a chef or simply developing a business structure around what you love to do for the purpose of using your influence to serve others. Now that is what should be your full-time work.

In subsequent chapters, more light will be shed on how to properly package your gifts. You may not be deploying your gifts appropriately because they are not well developed and branded.

For example, some people are naturally funny. Anything they say is hilarious. When some comedians appear on the stage or in a movie, people burst into laughter, even before they say a word. Maybe you are endowed with the same talents and you are just making people laugh for free, and for fun. Nurture your gift, package, and rebrand it and entertain people with it so that people can laugh off stress from their life especially at this time of global "gloom and doom."

In return, you will be richly rewarded because you would have been turned into an ambassador of joy. Research findings show that during the economic meltdown, hollywood is still soaring high because people who are stressed want to have fun and chill out. Again, nobody can fire you from yourself. Your job is your career. Your work is your life's assignment. Your job is temporary, your company or organization could go belly-up; your core gift remains with you. Your work is permanent; your job reveals your superficial self because you are trained to act professionally. You are taught to smile at everyone, most especially to your clients, although deep within, you might not like what you are doing. Your work is your real self, that's the real you. Your job could be your means of livelihood whereas your work is your source of fortune.

If you work hard on your job, your income only increases by some percentages, but if you put in more effort into your work, your fortune becomes generational. It is okay to earn a five or six figure salary if you are working on a job, but I challenge you to hire yourself. You will derive fulfillment while walking in your divine purpose. It may not instantly bring you large sums of money, but in the end, you will be glad you did.

It is like a fish swimming conveniently in water because the body of water is its natural environment. You cannot disable the fish from swimming in water, except you kill it, so also no one can hinder you from manifesting your gift on earth. It should be a consistent, daily experience until your last breath.

Study Guide

1. Identify the four stages of human development.

   a.

   b.

   c.

   d.

2. Discuss with your study group the competence stage that is more relevant to your core gift.

3. If you had an audience with your hero who is so influential and he asks you to explain your most pressing desire in life, what would that be? Write it in two sentences below.

   a.

   b.

4. Identify three differences between your God-given purpose and your career.

   a.

   b.

   c.

5. No one can fire you from your work. Discuss why in the space below.

6. Discuss the main difference between your full-time work and your part-time job.

   a.

   b.

7. How far or close are you to the stage of unconscious competence in your core gift? If you think you are not close enough, what three efforts are you making?

   a.

   b.

   c.

Chapter 5

MULTIPLE INTELLIGENCES AND MULTI-GIFTEDNESS

Information Overload Debunked

We live in an age where an average person in search of meaning in life is constantly and aggressively being bombarded with information that is capable of causing an emotional and nervous breakdown. Even though information is crucial and highly needed in this day and age, the importance of adequate, relevant information relative to one's main goal in life should be the bedrock of any search, otherwise too much irrelevant information, also known as information overload which is the bane of the twenty-first century social and economic landscape, would be the order of the day. Information overload is defined as stress induced by reception of more information than is necessary to make a decision. It is a term popularized by Alvin Toffler, a researcher and writer, that explains the difficulty or challenge a person can have in trying to understand an issue and making decisions that can be caused by the presence of too much information.

> *Information overload is defined as stress induced by reception of more information than is necessary to make a decision.*

While it is necessary to gather relevant information on any issue before a major decision is made, it is also imperative to know that too much out-of-context information before a pro-active decision could lead to pressure that is capable of impairing one's productivity. It could leave the individual in a state of anomy. It is believed that the media, as informative and necessary as it is, disseminates more information that the seventeenth century man or woman would have encountered in a lifetime. It is also believed that there is enough scientific information written everyday to fill seven complete sets of Encyclopedia Britannica.

A recent study shows that information created annually through books, digital devices, e-mails, blogs, and web pages is virally growing at an alarming rate of over 70 percent. The danger of this trend is, if it is not well managed, such a plethora of information bombardment has the propensity to paralyze the psychology and even the physiology of its recipient. Another danger posed by information overload is the ever increasing presence of ADS (Attention Disorder Syndrome) being experienced by some people who have challenges with maintaining focus by succeeding at one thing first which Herbert Simon, a Psychologist says could lead to "a wealth of information creates a poverty of attention..." What a paradox! My thesis throughout this book is simple and it cannot be overemphasized: focus and gather enough information relevant to your main intelligence or core gift, develop them and systematically deploy them as you pursue your God-ordered purpose. You can never know everything. Ignore irrelevant information.

Therefore, this chapter focuses on the many confusions and frustrations associated with multiple talents or intelligences and how to navigate through them by focusing on the main thing, thus making the main thing the main thing.

Maybe you have been distracted or you are being tempted to be distracted; I feel you. Because of God's multiple abilities on my life, I have done many things successfully, but not necessarily effectively. From pastoring to itinerant ministry, to co-founding a multi-million dollar business, to marketing as an executive for fortune 500 Inc. companies, I know what it means for a man to spread himself too thin when he has so many things on his plate.

The challenge is that, he may be successful but may not be able to consolidate his success because he will be overwhelmed, come under pressure, and everything may fall apart if he does not address what is most important to him. This is my honest story in a nutshell which I do not regret because I have since realized that my pain could be somebody else's gain.

My story of frustration and struggle is somebody else's navigation out of confusion which is one of the main reasons for this book in your hands. God did not make a mistake by endowing you with several talents and gifts at the same time. In fact, studies show that an average person has more than one core gift. Some have multiple core gifts. That in itself is not a minus but a plus provided the individual learns how to transition effectively which I did not know because I had not been taught or maybe there were no authors writing along these areas, especially Christian authors which are usually most Christians' favorites. So I took it as a challenge to start a movement in this arena.

Searching through the Bible, I discovered that the greatest individuals God used were multi-talented people. Apostle Paul could relate when he said, "This one thing I do..." You could know what a man is struggling from or what he has mastered through what he emphasizes every time he speaks or writes. I believe Paul had to say that to remind himself of the need to be laser focused on his main calling in life.

Let's look at a few heroes of faith, including Jesus Christ, who had to focus on their main, core gifts regardless of the others but learned how to use the other gifts as complements without allowing their core gifts to be submerged.

Jesus Christ: Carpenter, healer, deliverer, His core gift (Savior)

Peter: Fisherman, swimmer, businessman, core gift (Preacher/Apostle)

Paul: Tentmaker, lawyer, Pharisee, core gift (Preacher/Apostle)

Luke: Physician, writer, core gift (Preacher/Apostle)

Moses: Shepherd, speaker (Acts 7:22), core gift (Deliverer)

Joseph: Dreamer, interpreter of dreams, administrator, core gift (dream and administration)

David: Fighter, singer, deliverer, song writer, harp player, core gift (Deliverer/Musician)

It is imperative for me to first let you know that historically, Bible heroes who lived at different dispensations operated in multiple gifts even before modern Scientists and Psychologists discovered a twenty-first century language to discuss their classifications. Empirically, the

Holy Bible therefore becomes the premise on which the theory of multiple intelligences (gift) is founded.

MULTIPLE INTELLIGENCES AND THE BIBLE

The theory of multiple intelligences was developed in 1983 by a Harvard professor of education, Dr. Howard Gardner, who also had a background in seminary. Without trying to be too academically complex, his basic premise is that it is unfair to categorize people and label them unintelligent based on the traditional status-quo of IQ testing. He suggested that the notion could be myopic and parochial.

The theory suggests that human beings can be grouped into seven different types of intelligences that could potentially account for a broader range of achieving intellectual participation of both children and adults in shaping human history. David alluded to this claim in the Bible when he said, *"I will praise You, for I am fearfully and wonderfully made..."* (Ps. 139:14). My attempt in this chapter is to underscore the universality and the parallel of divine, multi- giftedness and psychological explanation of the theory of multiple intelligences.

Do not forget my proposition that every branch of so-called secular knowledge is rooted in the Bible. Therefore, this chapter attempts to juxtapose my scriptural findings in relation to the theory.

EIGHT BASIC INTELLIGENCES

Linguistic Intelligence: People who are word smart. They are sensitive to spoken and written language. They have the ability to learn languages and have the capacity to use language to accomplish certain goals. People in this group include; preachers, professional speakers, attorneys, journalists, writers, poets, playwrights, artists, politicians, etc. Bible Findings: All the writers of the four synoptic gospels (Matthew, Mark, Luke, and John), Paul the Apostle etc. So, if you are good with words; such as speaking or writing, you are linguistically intelligent.

Logical–Mathematical Intelligence: This is the capacity to analyze problems logically, carry out mathematical operations and investigate issues scientifically. It is the ability to be rational, logical and analytical. People that would fit into this arena are scientists, mathematicians, doctors, accountants, etc. Bible Findings: Bezalel the architect who was imparted by Moses and was instrumental in building the temple.

"(30)And Moses said to the children of Israel, "See, the LORD has called by name Bezalel the son of Uri, the son of Hur, of the tribe of Judah; (31)and He has filled him with the Spirit of God, in wisdom and understanding, in knowledge and all manner of workmanship, (32) to design artistic works, to work in gold and silver and bronze, (33)in cutting jewels for setting, in carving wood, and to work in all manner of artistic workmanship (Exod. 35:30-33).

Musical Intelligence: This is the capacity to compose, perform and appreciate music. This could also intertwine with linguistic intelligence. People with musical intelligence include singers, song writers, musicians, etc. Bible Findings: David, the Levites, etc. Also, remember the musician who had to set the atmosphere right for the man of God to function effectively in his prophetic gift? (2 Kings 3:11-16).

Bodily-Kinesthetic Intelligence: This is the ability and potential to use one's body or parts of the body to solve problems. It is the capacity to use abilities to co-ordinate bodily movements. The people in this group include sports men and women in various sports like football, tennis, soccer, basketball, swimming, etc. Bible Findings: David; when he ran after the lion and the bear before killing them. He did a similar thing before killing Goliath with his sling. Are you good in any sport or do you like to use your hands like an artisan, then this is your intelligence.

Spatial Intelligence: The ability to recognize and use wide space and more confined space to your advantage. People in this category are architects, interior decorators. Bible Findings: Bezalel (Exod. 38:1-7). If you have the ability to manage space efficiently and creatively bring out the beauty that others cannot see, this may be your intelligence.

Interpersonal Intelligence: This is the capacity to understand the intentions, motivations and desires of other people. It allows people to efficiently relate with others. People in this arena include ministers of the gospel, religious leaders, sales people, psychologists, political leaders, etc. Bible Findings: Almost all the kings and the patriarchs, the judges and the disciples of Jesus Christ in the Bible. If you are naturally good at relating with people and you get along well, this could be the intelligence that you need to focus on more.

Intra-Personal Intelligence: This is the capacity to understand one's self, feelings, fears, motivations, and boundaries. People in this group include lone rangers who like to work independently. Intercessors, mothers raising their children, and those whose callings are private often fall into this category. If you like your privacy or like to be in the background, this may be your unique intelligence. Bible findings: Most of the prophets in the bible will likely be in this group. They were either in the desert or on the mountain alone with God.

Supernatural Intelligence (My discovery): Even though psychologists and behavioral scientists will not endorse it because of what they might call its lack of ability to be substantiated by scientific study, it is however a reality. This is because the realm of the spirit is more real than the realm of the natural. Supernatural intelligence can be defined as the ability to possibly engage in any endeavor covering all aspects of human life with a view to helping people through an empowerment that is beyond the realm of the physical. It is called the anointing of the Holy Spirit or the grace of God. All the anointed men and women that God used in the Bible functioned in the category of supernatural intelligence. Elisha, for example, through supernatural, security intelligence, was able to reveal certain plots against the King of Israel many times. The King was divinely protected from being assassinated because Elisha was able to function beyond the realm of the natural to see what the enemies were planning (1 Kings 6:8-12).

Jesus Christ remains the undeniable embodiment of all types of intelligence including the spiritual one. He walked on the water, healed many diseases, fed thousands spiritually and raised many people from the dead.

Interestingly, because He is not a leader with ego and esteem problems, He takes delight in His disciples doing far greater than Him. His injunction in John 14:12 *"...greater work than these you will do..."* is coming to pass all over the world today. Nations are being swept with the miracle-working power of the Holy Spirit. I believe the end has not yet come because some of the major characters in this current move of supernatural intelligence are "special people," Apostles, Evangelists, Prophets, Pastors, and Teachers. The world is still waiting for the "ordinary people" to come to the center stage of this move. Can you imagine "maids, servants," and other domestic staff prophesying? It would happen on a massive scale. We are very close (Joel 2:28-30).

These people and others that I have seen in certain villages in Africa may not be able to display any of the other intelligences but they are super, spiritually intelligent. My whole thesis in this chapter especially with the concept of supernatural intelligence is to destroy the philosophy of disparaging anyone who may not be able to function effectively in the other seven intelligences or label them "not smart enough." The only thing some people may be able to do effectively in their entire life is prayer. Now how do you explain that scientifically?

> *My whole thesis in this chapter especially with the concept of supernatural intelligence is to destroy the philosophy of disparaging anyone who may not be able to function effectively in the other seven intelligences or label them "not smart enough."*

So, if your intelligence is supernatural or intangible, DO NOT be discouraged or trivialize it. We need you more than ever before in these last days especially when the devil is attacking the church with the spirit of humanism, which in my opinion is the greatest threat to the preaching of the cross. However, the preaching of the cross will prevail because you can't preach the cross without talking about the blood which is usually the last card the devil hates (Revelation 12:11). I discussed this 8th intelligence more vividly in part five "The Apocalypse." It should be noted, just like the multi-giftedness counterpart of this discussion, people could have a blend of intelligences.

In *Frames of Mind*, Howard Gardner postulates "...people could have a unique blend of intelligences... but the big challenge facing the deployment of human resources is how to best take advantage of the uniqueness conferred on us as a species exhibiting several intelligences." I personally believe that a self-discovery of who you are, your abilities and limitations through the grace of God would prevent you from having a nebulous fantasy of the world and reduce instantaneous euphoria that is usually associated with emotional hypes. Dr. Gardner further says, "I want my children to understand the world, but not just because the world is fascinating and the human mind is curious. I want them to understand it so that they will be positioned to make it a better place. Knowledge is not the same as morality but we need to understand it if we are to avoid past mistakes and move in productive directions. An important part of that understanding is knowing who we are and what we can do."

Another psychologist that has contributed immensely to the study and development of multiple intelligences is Dr. Thomas Armstrong who wrote *7 Kinds of Smart: Identifying and Developing Your Many Intelligences*. Just like Armstrong and Gardener, my contribution is hinged on one fact: that people should not be labeled "dull" or "not smart" because of their inability to display certain intelligences or abilities. In fact, the original vision behind the concept of multiple intelligences was to help the school systems pay attention to the diverse, innate potentials of each child based on the type of intelligence they display. However, unfortunately, certain children who may not be able to exhibit the linguistic intelligence or the logical, mathematical intelligence are often looked down upon as not "smart enough" and in certain extreme cases labeled ADD (Attention Deficit Disorder).

The theory believes that maybe a careful examination of their traits and idiosyncrasies might just reveal that they are talented in other areas of intelligence like spatial or bodily kinesthetic. I believe that there are even many adults today who are probably working in certain endeavors that imprison them because those fields are at variance with their unique intelligences. Could that be one of the reasons why Jesus would use different images, parables, examples like farm products, fishes, crops, animals and contextual allegories to explain eternal truths to His immediate audience? They basically comprised of people in the fishing and dairy business. I bet you, Jesus Christ would have used TV, computer and other digital devices to teach the gospel of the kingdom today.

My main objective in this chapter is using different approaches to explain the same fundamental truth about how loaded you are. If you relate better with spiritual idioms, I hope you are comfortable with words like gifts or talents. If however, you prefer academic engagement, I hope the multiple intelligences theory fits for you. The point is, it is just an issue of semantics. Today's scholars are only trying to unravel age long, Bible truths, and that's okay provided the truth is not distorted in the process.

Study Guide

1. Identify four unique gifts you have and their importance to you.
   a.

   b.

   c.

   d.

2. If you were to combine two of them, which two would you put together?

3. What do you think is your main intelligence after studying the eight intelligences?

4. Discuss four main talents you have and group them under the appropriate intelligence.

   Talents

   1.

   2.

   3.

   4.

   Intelligence

   1.

   2.

   3.

   4.

Part Two

THE SILENT YEARS

Chapter 6

THE EAGLE'S EYE

Making the Main Thing, the Main Thing

At the fiftieth wedding anniversary of Henry Ford, journalists asked him, "Mr. Ford, what is the secret of your successful marriage?" "Sticking to the same model" was his short, but firm answer. Allan Mulally, the current CEO of Ford has adopted the same philosophy. It is called Intensity of Focus. The auto giant bounced back from almost getting a bankruptcy and refusing to take tax payer bailout money. They had a whooping 6.6 billion dollars in net income in 2010. This is significant for a company that four years before was struggling from a 12.7 billion dollar loss.

The new CEO's business plan is based on a simple slogan, "One Ford." In fact, it is so simple that critics call it "silly," but you cannot argue with result. This philosophy adopted by Mulally is not new to the company, it has been re-engineered to keep up with the current challenges but the tradition of intensity of focus remains the same.

Ability to maintain focus and make the main thing, the main thing is not only a requirement for making progress in any life's endeavors, it also helps you to keep your sanity. It enables you to get better at the particular thing you are called to do thereby sharpening your core competence.

Ability to maintain focus and make the main thing, the main thing is not only a requirement for making progress in any life's endeavors, it also helps you to keep your sanity.

"There are many plans in a man's heart, Nevertheless the LORD's counsel—that will stand" (Prov. 19:21).

Some people are versatile, like I examined in the last chapter, but end up accomplishing little because they have not been able to improve their skills in a particular sphere of life. The seemingly appealing gifts can be their undoing in the race of life because they are caught up in life's everyday hustle and bustle, trying to provide answers to every life issue at the expense of discovering and fulfilling their life assignment.

Human beings brainstorm diverse options and plans because of their different abilities, but it is the very purpose of God that should prevail. It is a wise thing to inquire about that will of your Creator for your life because that is the main basis for your existence on earth. Paul, the apostle, a man of great intellect and various abilities, had an understanding of this when he sought the Lord to know Him more. Although he had encountered the Lord Jesus Christ, he became exceptionally inquisitive regarding a deeper understanding of God's unique plan for his life.

When he obtained a substantial part of it, he counted all his past achievement as history, and his goal was to attain the destiny which had been ordained for him.

"(10)that I may know Him and the power of His resurrection, and the fellowship of His sufferings, being conformed to His death, (12)Not that I have already attained, or am already perfected; but I press on, that I may lay hold of that for which Christ Jesus has also laid hold of me. (13) Brethren, I do not count myself to have apprehended; but one thing I do, forgetting those things which are behind and reaching forward to those things which are ahead, (14)I press toward the goal for the prize of the upward call of God in Christ Jesus" (Phil. 3:10, 12-14).

Though your divine purpose and gift can be intertwined, they are not necessarily the same. As I mentioned earlier, if just singing is purpose in itself, then most singers should be over fulfilled by now, but that is not the case. A lot of them are depressed because their talents have been perverted from what they were designed to accomplish.

Multi-giftedness has been a hindrance to some in the journey of purpose because they have been distracted from the main reason for living. You are not here on earth to merely display your gifts but to use them specifically for the fulfillment of your purpose. God might have endowed you with several abilities, but understanding how to make them effective and relevant for the enhancement of your divine assignment is paramount. The truth of the matter is, every one of us has the ability to actually do many things at the same time, the only problem is, can we be effective doing that? You can only be efficient when you focus on one main thing at a time. For example, many people can cook, but how many can cook well while watching the television? The divided attention will drastically reduce the efficiency of their cooking skill.

In the same manner, countless gifted people are being rendered ineffective because of their involvement in too many activities to the detriment of the main thing, their earthly assignment. I have personally explored a couple of career paths such as professional marketing and startup business developments. I was greatly rewarded for my outstanding contributions to those companies, but I had to quit at some point. It was necessary for me so that I could be more devoted to my divine purpose, and I have no regrets whatsoever for my decision.

Though I acquired experience in the process of accomplishing many duties, I was distracted for a period of time because of too much pressure.

CORE GIFT VERSUS OTHER ABILITIES

I adumbrated a few Bible heroes who had various gifts in the last chapter. For the sake of emphasis, I will explain the difference between their core gift and their other talents. It is pertinent to do this because a lot of people get stuck with knowing exactly what to do with multiple abilities.

Paul, the Apostle: The story of Paul in the Scriptures shows that he went through a period when he struggled to do many things at the same time, but in the long run he was able to focus on the main reason for his existence on earth. This gifted man was a Pharisee, lawyer, and tent-maker, but his main focus was his calling as an apostle to the gentiles. He traded away everything to do just that, which could be one of the reasons why he said; *"…this one thing I do."*

There is nothing wrong in doing many things at the same time but the mastery of the main thing, the gifts associated with your divine purpose is beneficial so that you can finish your assignment excellently and be approved by God. Focusing on the main or dominant gift will facilitate your journey to that purpose.

Many Christians pray and fast for financial breakthroughs. While it is spiritual and godly to pray, but the truth is, breakthroughs can't be obtained doing many things at the same time. Also, doing the wrong thing may only lead to little or no success. Even when you do know your vision, you still need to be focused. Paul, a man of diverse abilities, had been through it all and because of his understanding, he advised, *"Let all things be done decently and in order"* (1 Corinthians 14:40). He was successful in many respects. He had a little success while building tents and also accomplished a relatively, comparable success in his legal profession until he discovered his core mission on earth. He considered everything as loss and pursued passionately that one thing and as a result, became a blessing to his world.

Jesus Christ: Our Lord grew and apparently learned the carpentry trade from His earthly father, Joseph. He introduced Himself with many words at different times, like when He said, *"I am the Way, the Truth and the Life."* At other times He called Himself *"the Bread of Life,"* and *"the Living Water."* The all-encompassing word that describes His mission on earth is "Savior."

That is why we Christians call Him the Savior, because His mission is to *"...save His people from their sins"* (Matthew 1:21). The word "Savior" captures His entire purpose in life. Since He was sure of His identity and assignment, He went about preaching the gospel of the kingdom thereby healing people of every ailment, setting them free from the hold of satan and opening their eyes to see the excellent way to live.

Jesus perfectly completed His earthly assignment when He eventually died on the cross and rose from the dead. He was able to achieve all these because He rightly channeled His gifts in the direction of His ultimate purpose.

Luke, the Apostle: Luke was an early Christian writer who was said to be the author of the Gospel of Luke and the Acts of the Apostles. Christian records also indicate that he was the first icon painter. He was said to have painted pictures of the virgin Mary, Peter, and Paul. In addition, archaeology accounts illustrate that Luke was a historian of the first rank; because of his trustworthy record which contributed immensely to the groundwork of Christian historical studies.

He was also a physician, but his dominant gift was to be an Apostle of Jesus Christ. He directed his gifts appropriately giving a detailed account of the life of his Master, Jesus, and also the early church.

Simon Peter: This apostle was a good swimmer being a fisherman. He loved fishing so much that he went back to it when Jesus died for three days.

He was an entrepreneur because when he caught a great number of fish after yielding to Jesus' instructions, asked his business partners to help out with the mighty breakthroughs. While Jesus was walking by the Sea of Galilee, He transformed Peter and his brother, Andrew, into fishers of men after recognizing their passion and dedication to their fishing business.

Peter heeded the call and focused his prevailing gift of apostleship on his life towards his assignment.

Moses: He was a powerful speaker because of the privilege of a solid education in Egypt, the most civilized country of his time. He became a shepherd when he fled to the wilderness to save his life from Pharaoh, the king of Egypt who wanted to destroy him for killing an Egyptian. At the back side of the desert, he was responsible for keeping the flock of Jethro, his father-in-law.

The turning point of his life came when he had an encounter with God at the burning bush that was not consumed. As he moved closer to the bush that was not razed by the fire, God spoke to him. He instantly started stuttering when God was commissioning him to deliver His people from their taskmaster. Who wouldn't? Can you imagine God sending you to a place where you have been declared wanted with a price tag on your head? He had not always stuttered.

"And Moses was learned in all the wisdom of the Egyptians, and was mighty in words and deeds" (Acts 7:22).

In the course of the conversation, God told him that his brother Aaron would be his mouth piece so that His purpose would not be hampered by any excuse. Everything Moses experienced in these different stages of his life helped prepare him for his main assignment of a deliverer. He effectively pastored four million people for a while just like he did to the sheep in his care while under the mentorship of Jethro.

What you are going through now may be the necessary preparation for the main assignment which God will entrust into your hands. You need to understand and begin to see everything as working together for your good. This is why you should not regret, complain or get depressed about all the things you have been involved in.

> *What you are going through now may be the necessary preparation for the main assignment which God will entrust into your hands.*

I thank God for everything I learned in marketing and the business world. My exposure to different kinds of people in the corporate marketplace is something I cannot trade for anything because it has allowed me to see how people think and relate in the real world. If I am going to effectively pastor real people and not angels, it just makes sense for me to identify with them. This is especially important for people like me who went straight into "full-time" ministry immediately after graduation from college. These experiences are now helping me in my pastoral calling because I now have to deal with people who are experiencing an array of challenges in different areas.

Don't focus on your present challenges, but rather approach every situation with a good attitude because it could just be a training phase of your life. God will usher you into new territories if you are faithful in what He has presently assigned to you. Remember the Bible says that;

> *"Whatever your hand finds to do, do it with your might; for there is no work or device or knowledge or wisdom in the grave where you are going"* (Eccles. 9:10).

> *"And whatever you do, do it heartily, as to the Lord and not to men"* (Col. 3:23).

You limit yourself when you focus so much on what you don't have but rather, be sensitive to the Holy Spirit by investing quality time with your Creator so that you can know what to focus on in every phase of your life as you journey along the path of destiny.

David: He is known as a man after God's heart. This special king was an acclaimed warrior, a musician, dancer and poet. He was credited with composing many of the psalms. Whenever the evil spirit troubled King Saul, David took a harp and played with his hand to drive away the evil spirit so that Saul could be refreshed. Also, according to the book of kings, David majored in fighting battles.

This gift was developed and perfected when he faithfully looked after the sheep and in the process conquered lions and bears. This emboldened him to face Goliath. He also effectively applied the same gift to conquer his enemies which surrounded him while he was the king of Israel. His ability to sing opened doors for him to minister in the palace, but it was not sufficient enough to help him rule successfully. He was ordained and anointed as a king. He marshaled his unusual ability to defend the helpless, risked his life in the process and blazed the trail for others to follow.

Myself: I have the natural ability to persuade people and efficiently applied this gift when I was involved in marketing. Once, I was involved in a sales negotiation, and after closing the deal, my wife said, "Sam Ore, you are very persuasive!" My dominant gift is communication whether through speaking or writing but my God-given purpose is to preach the gospel of the kingdom in every part of the world using various media. To be more precise, my vision in life is to help other people achieve theirs. My brand is empowerment. God's unique ability on my life helps me pass my message across to my intended audience with clarity.

I am now able to deploy it in the direction of my purpose because I developed it while I was in the marketing profession in the secular world. I have not arrived yet, but it gets better for me every day as I focus on the main thing. As you increase the capacity of your gift by using it to boost your purpose, uncommon opportunities will come your way to express your other gifts and this will attract the right resources and competent people to manage them for you without you being personally involved.

You: Fill in the blank. This chapter is not complete without you.

_____

_____

_____

_____

_____

Study Guide

---

1. Identify three main differences between your core gift and your purpose.

   a.

   b.

   c.

2. In certain cases, gifts and purpose are closely intertwined. Discuss this expression with your study group.

3. It has been said that an average person has more than one gift. Identify yours.

   a.

   b.

   c.

   d.

   e.

4. Which of the gifts above are you currently developing? And why?

5. In three sentences, explain why multi-giftedness could be counterproductive if not well managed.

   a.

   b.

   c.

6. Discuss with your accountability partner two multi-gifted Bible characters who successfully engaged their main gifts to fulfill their God-given purpose.

   a.

   b.

Chapter 7

THE POWER OF SIMPLICITY

Uncluttering your Core Gift

In the last chapter, we examined the importance of focusing on the main thing. While this sounds simple, and so profoundly important, yet it is one of the most difficult issues facing the majority of people in their journey to purpose. However, you can only concentrate or deliberately focus on your core ability or gift only when you recognize them. If you think you are multi-gifted like most people, it is imperative that you do an honest, objective evaluation of your abilities in the light of the following questions. Please pay closer attention to the word MOST. Observing the word MOST could make a significant difference in those questions. As simple as it sounds, it could also be the cardinal, revealing difference between this chapter and similar ones you have read in other books. There are eight main recommended questions you should ask yourself. You need to be honest, objective, and pay attention to the word MOST in those questions. My repetition of the word "most" should not bore you. It is deliberate because I really want it to resonate with you. Paying attention to the word MOST could make a life-changing difference in those questions.

Question 1: In whatever you do currently, whether it is a job, a profession, school or a combination of many things, where are you MOST effective? Not where you are toiling or laboring more. You can be busy without being efficient or effective.

Question 2: What ability excites you MOST consistently? Many things can get people excited at the same time depending on their temperament, seasons or stages of their life. For instance, a young lady who is about to be married to her heartthrob is supposed to be happy about that season of her life. But the dominant gift that creates a particular energy in your life is not seasonal. It is always consistent.

Question 3: What infuriates you MOST? The problem you see every time and the crisis that upsets you every time MOST is the problem you have been created to solve. The question is: what core gift do you constantly use when solving such problems? King David was so smart when confronted by Goliath. He used his most strategic gift and weapon. It is not wise to experiment with the gift you have not mastered in the face of major crisis.

Question 4: If you are experiencing some degree of success presently in your endeavors, what gift or ability is MOSTLY responsible? Not the job or the profession or the business or whatever you are doing. Otherwise, if that were the case, everybody doing similar things should automatically be successful in that endeavor; but you and I know that is neither the case nor reality. It is the gift, talent or ability in that profession that makes you stand out. The job or profession could just be the platform to display your core gift. Joseph was a slave boy in Potiphar's house (his job), but his administrative gift made him succeed, not necessarily the job title or description. The same administrative gift made room for him in the prison when he was made to supervise the other prisoners. The gift of interpretation of dreams opened the door to the king, while the same gift of administration inspired him to write a proposal and finally established him in his purpose (Government). Some of the most successful pastors I have met may not necessarily be great speakers, but majority of them do have the gift of administration or some measure of organizational skills.

Question 5: What is the gift or ability that the people around you refer to MOST? Sometimes, God uses other people as witnesses of His manifold grace upon people's life. *"By the mouth of two or three witnesses every word shall be established"* (2 Corinthians 13:1). These people could be your clients, customers, students, church members, mentors, protégées, pastors and even parents. If you work in a boutique shop for instance and you always consistently outsell other sales people because you are cheerful and make friends easily, God could be giving you a clue to develop the gift of making friends into a system that could benefit the company you work for by writing a proposal that would take the company to another level. You could just ask for equity ownership of a certain percentage, except you want to start your own business. A word of caution: even though I am huge on people starting their own businesses, I am discovering that the reality of life is that not everybody will own an independent business. The best some people can do is having a stake in an organization and they will just be fine. I look at the different concepts related to this in another chapter.

Question 6: Where do you always experience a sense of destiny the MOST? Anytime you want to retire to bed after using or engaging different abilities, gifts or passions during the day, which of them can you honestly say "I was born to do this." I personally made some good money as a senior vice president of a telecom company, but there has been nothing like what I am doing right now.

Question 7: If you have five minutes to live, what is the ONE thing you will do, and what is the ONE particular gift you will most likely engage in the process? If you can identify that ONE thing, that is your purpose in life. If you can identify that ONE particular gift you will use to accomplish it, that will be your core intelligence.

Question 8: If money or any material rewards were not an issue, what gift would you use MOST to help people solve their problems? Whatever gift you will use for free before realizing that you are not getting paid is the core gift for your purpose. In other words, if money were never to be a problem for you for the rest of your life, what is going to be your daily lifestyle? Imagine your entire bill paid and all your needs and luxuries met, what will you be doing with your life to help people? If you can truly and sincerely recognize that ONE thing, that will be your God-given purpose. I had to sincerely ask myself this question at a point "Suppose I am making a billion dollars every month, will I still be preaching?" I honestly knew within my heart that my life will be off-course and empty if I quit preaching. If I had felt otherwise, I will be the first person to announce to everybody I know that I quit. I think one of the greatest misnomers in the church today is to give people the impression that they don't have a purpose unless they are doing what looks "spiritual." By spiritual, I mean the five-fold ministry gift of apostles, prophets, evangelists, pastors and teachers. This impression is misleading.

COMPETING WITH YOURSELF

It is a relative statement to say that a particular person is the best in a particular vocation. It depends on what you are focusing on because if you ask some of the world's famous speakers to give a talk on a subject they are not familiar with, they would probably perform below average. For example, most people believe that President Barack Obama is a great speaker, I also do, but it would be wrong to say he is the best speaker in the world. That would be a general, absolute statement. (Statements that are made in absolute terms are usually subjective for the most part).

This is because I don't think he has the capability to speak as a sport commentator and if he attempts it, he may not be as impressive as he appears in his natural habitat, which is politics.

Some preachers specialize in eschatology or other end-time events because that is their passion. I cannot preach excellently in every area of life, but when it comes to empowering people and showing them how to reign in their calling, I feel much more at home. You can't just generalize but you have to focus on a particular area in order to properly access the expert in you.

For example, it is subjective to say that Tiger Woods is the best sportsman in the world because he can only be compared to other golf players to know if he's actually the best or not. Lionel Messi from Argentina who plays as a center forward cannot be regarded as the best soccer player in the world, but he can be the best entertaining soccer player in the world because of his unique speed and skill of dribbling. You cannot compare midfielders with goalkeepers. Neither can you compare defenders with attackers. Their roles are fundamentally different even though they are playing the same sport. So, stop comparing yourself with others. Compete with yourself. This world has been described as a big drama stage where everybody plays his or her role. Some will play major roles, while others will play minor parts. Every character is important so as to sustain the plot. In Act 9:36 for example, a woman named Dorcas is referred to as a "disciple," a term used to describe the apostles of Jesus Christ. Her purpose was so simple that it could be ignored. She met the needs of the widows by providing clothes for them. Her core competence for achieving that was fashion designing. Joseph of Arimathea is also described as a "disciple" whose purpose was to preserve the body of the Lord Jesus in a befitting tomb. His core intelligence was probably government or business. He leveraged his influence to approach the government who allowed him to take Jesus' body away for burial. Peter and the other apostles with their very attractive, flamboyant apostolic gift, couldn't have done that.

The notion that everybody must be famous to indicate how relevant they are in God's agenda is not only misleading, but myopic. This kind of mindset has the propensity to put people under pressure that are capable of causing emotional, roller- coaster-experience and avoidable hallucinations. I am of a strong opinion that some people's purpose in life could just be to work behind the scene while making other people famous for God. In the final analysis, only God knows exactly who is great and who is popular with Him. Therefore, compete with yourself.

> *The notion that everybody must be famous to indicate how relevant they are in God's agenda is not only misleading, but myopic. This kind of mindset has the propensity to put people under pressure that are capable of causing emotional, roller-coaster-experience and avoidable hallucinations.*

TURNING YOUR WEAKNESSES INTO STRENGTHS

There is a general saying that in order to be successful, you have to work on your weaknesses. Regarding moral issues, yes. It is good to continually work on your weaknesses so that you can develop a godly character. Even this can't be done by will power but by depending solely on Jesus Christ, the author and finisher of your faith.

The more you struggle to become holy, the more sinful you become. The way to victorious living is to sincerely ask Jesus Christ to strengthen you with His grace, and then it becomes easier for you to develop godly character. However, in the area of skills or gifts, no. Do not work on your weakness. When I was in high school, for instance, my weakness was mathematics because I didn't want to get involved with anything that had to do with numbers. I was very good in English language and literature but I was always advised to keep working on my quantitative skills at the expense of developing my verbal skills. This is the reason why some of the industrialized countries of the world have made more progress than some developing countries. Let's go back to sports; Tiger Woods is ranked among the most successful golfers of all time.

Playing golf is his strength and he gets better in it as he practices often. Doing this enables him to sharpen his strengths until he becomes almost perfect in it. Kim Clijsters, a citizen of Belgium is rated among the greatest in her field of professional tennis. In this hypothetical example, golf will be her weakness. It would be foolish of her to start working on her weakness because she is already without struggle as an expert in playing tennis.

In the same way, it would be a waste of time for Tiger Woods to start learning how to be a professional in tennis. Working on your strengths makes you better, until you become the best because practice makes perfect. That statement is true when you practice only your strengths. God knows who you are and what you can handle. Your weakness can never intimidate Him, therefore focus on your strength and practice until the whole world comes to celebrate the gift of God in your life. In moral issues, working on your weakness through the grace of God is proper, but when it comes to your gift, working on your strength (core gift) makes perfection while working on your weakness (what you are not wired for) makes permanent.

> *In moral issues, working on your weakness through the grace of God is proper, but when it comes to your gift, working on your strength (core gift) makes perfection while working on your weakness (what you are not wired for) makes permanent.*

Study Guide

---

1. List four areas where you are most gifted in their order of importance.

   a.

   b.

   c.

   d.

2. Write three memorable things you have accomplished within the last three years. What are the gifts mostly responsible for your success?

   Events

   a.

   b.

   c.

   Gift responsible

   a.

   b.

   c.

3. Identify three areas of strength (gift).

   a.

   b.

   c.

4. Identify three areas of weakness (what you don't have the ability to do).

   a.

   b.

   c.

5. If you had five minutes left on earth, what problem would you
    want to solve?

6. Write down three things you hate to see around.

    a.

    b.

    c.

7. What are you going to do about those problems in #6 above starting
    today?

8. What are your three pro-active strategies?

    a.

    b.

    c.

Chapter 8

PRO-ACTIVE TARGET PRACTICE

Putting Pressure on Your Core Intelligence

"(13)Till I come, give attention to reading, to exhortation, to doctrine. (14)Do not neglect the gift that is in you, which was given to you by prophecy with the laying on of the hands of the eldership. (15)Meditate on these things; give yourself entirely to them, that your progress may be evident to all" (1 Tim. 4:13-15).

"(6)Therefore I remind you to stir up the gift of God which is in you through the laying on of my hands. (7)For God has not given us a spirit of fear, but of power and of love and of a sound mind" (2 Tim. 1:6-7).

For a long time, I believe these Scriptures have been wrongly quoted by many because they have not taken a closer look at them. The two Scriptures above are making reference to the gift of God in you. The word "gift" in the two Scriptures is singular, referring to your dominant grace. Whenever you attempt to stir up the gift, to do something meaningful with it, the devil will want to stop you. For this core gift to be activated, meditation of God's word needs to be taken seriously.

Meditation on God's Word is time spent with God. Like all relationships, time invested helps make it stronger and more intimate. Meditation taps into a source of blessing that goes beyond the natural world. It allows you to tap into the very life of God as you get closer to Him.

The core gift that is dormant in you will be activated when you are full of that life. When the gift is stirred up, it is your responsibility to use it purposefully to help others and duly get rewarded for it here in this world. According to the Greek lexicon, the word "gift" in both

Scriptures is from a Greek word, "Charisma," meaning "gift of or from God," or "favored by God."

It is God's unmerited favor and it has nothing to do with what you have done. It has nothing to do with your education, background, and social class. So, you cannot earn it. It is a trait found in individuals whose personalities are inherently characterized by a powerful attractiveness, along with intelligent, sophisticated abilities of interpersonal communication and influence.

One who is charismatic is said to be capable of using his personal being, rather than just speech or logic alone, to interface with other human beings in a personal and direct manner, and effectively communicate an argument or concept to them. It is simply an amazing display of the grace of God. Everyone born into this world has at least one gift from God.

In addition, everything you will ever need to fulfill your God-given purpose, no matter how difficult it may appear, has been provided for in Christ Jesus. With the help of the Holy Spirit, you have to go all the way to physically obtain them because they are your rightful inheritance. Every prayer we pray to God in the name of Jesus on any matter receives instant response from His throne room.

In answering these prayers, God works through people and circumstances. It is therefore necessary to always walk in love with everyone because they could be the answer to your prayer in certain areas. Everything you will ever need in this life to make an impact, whether it is spiritual, human or material resources has been provided for when Jesus gave up His spirit and said, *"It is finished"* (John 19:30).

A good understanding of this profound point helps you overcome certain temporary setbacks you might encounter.

"Therefore let no one boast in men. For all things are yours" (1 Cor. 3:21).

"Do you see a man diligent and skillful in his business? He will stand before kings; he will not stand before obscure men" (Prov. 22:29).

The implication of this Scripture is, whatever gift God has endowed you with will always be relevant as long as people live on this planet.

The awareness of this is so important as you apply it to your divine assignment. It will also help you focus more and be diligent in your business.

"For I wish that all men were even as I myself. But each one has his own gift from God, one in this manner and another in that" (1 Cor. 7:7).

"For the gifts and the calling of God are irrevocable" (Rom. 11:29).

When you combine the two Scriptures, it means God created each one of us distinctively and has endowed each person with a gift that cannot be taken away from him or her. A lot of Christians have this misconception that if you sin, God will take away your gift.

I don't think so, even though I'm not in any way encouraging people to live in sin. It is to your advantage to live a consecrated life because the closer you are to God the more refined your gift becomes. If God withdraws His gift from you because you have made a mistake, then it's no longer grace because grace is unmerited favor. Remember one of the pillars in the anatomy of a God-given purpose is the permanent nature of His gift in people's life. The gifts of God are irrevocable (Romans 11:29). Even though this Scripture is contextually referring to Israel as a nation, it is also relevant here. You didn't do anything to earn it in the first place, but God in His mercy imparted it on you so that you could fulfill your earthly assignment with it.

TARGET PRACTICE

This gift of God comes to you in raw states, but needs to be refined. This is usually done by target practice as you intentionally and intensely put pressure on it. In the process, you sharpen and improve your gifts. Your developed gift will naturally bring you fame because people will come to you in droves when they are convinced that you have the keys to unravel their mysteries and bring them happiness. Our Creator is an excellent God and the closer you draw near to Him, the more excellent you and your gifts will become. In 1 Timothy 4: 10-14, the Scriptures we

> *This gift of God comes to you in raw states, but needs to be refined. This is usually done by target practice as you intentionally and intensely put pressure on it.*

began with, the impression is that there is no way you can hide excellence from anyone, *"… that your profit may appear to all…"*

The Greek word for "appear" is *kaneros*, which means to shine. Your gift is stirred up when you deeply meditate on it and put it to use, then your profiting will appear to all, meaning your success and progress will become visible to everyone.

For example, it is not possible for a pregnant woman to hide her pregnancy because of her protruding stomach which appears after some months, so also it is not possible to hide your fruitfulness after waiting on God for a long time through the meditation of His word.

The Greek word, *kaneros* also means "externally abroad," which means that God will perform some exploits through you that will be published externally abroad. Another meaning for *kaneros* is "glorious." The word, "glory" has multi-dimensional meanings. First, it means "radiance, brilliance and brightness." It is the intrinsic brilliance of God that is of necessity, and in a variety of ways, displayed and beheld.

Secondly, it means wealth, honor and respect. As you stir up your gift, God will gloriously direct resources to you for being a good steward of His gift in your life. As wealth is being drawn to you gloriously on every side, your life becomes honorable, because glory and honor walk hand in hand. In the book of Genesis, chapter 30, Jacob was employed by Laban, and his business experienced a boom because of the involvement of Jacob, the blessed man.

Later, Jacob realized that Laban was defrauding him and as a result, negotiated with him so that he could have part equity ownership after which he will start his own business. Laban indeed confessed to Jacob; *"…for I have learned by experience that the LORD has blessed me for your sake"* (Genesis 30:27).

This marked the turnaround and new beginning in Jacob's life. Then, he became exceedingly great (very wealthy) and his fame spread abroad. When Jacob left Laban's house, his children accused him of taking away all the glory (wealth) of their father. Everything in Jacob's possession was referred to as glory.

His camels, cattle, maidservants, men servants, his sons and daughters were referred to as "glory." All these material blessings came because Jacob was always putting pressure on his core gift of creative thinking.

What a gift! Also, when Solomon became very great, the queen of Sheba, who was also very wealthy, came to visit him to witness his glorious wisdom.

"(4)And when the queen of Sheba had seen all the wisdom of Solomon, the house that he had built, (5)the food on his table, the seating of his servants, the service of his waiters and their apparel, his cupbearers, and his entryway by which he went up to the house of the LORD, there was no more spirit in her" (1 Kings 10:4-5).

"(28)So why do you worry about clothing? Consider the lilies of the field, how they grow: they neither toil nor spin; (29)and yet I say to you that even Solomon in all his glory was not arrayed like one of these" (Matt. 6:28-29).

The queen almost gave up her spirit when she saw the glorious display of Solomon's wisdom. This was in the Old Testament but Jesus made reference to it while teaching His disciples in the Gospels. He described Solomon's wealth with the word "glory." This is another proof that Glory (wealth) is not a sin because the Bible says that in the mouths of two or three witnesses every word will be established. All these so called anti-prosperity messages are not only erroneous, but ludicrous. Though, it has to be preached with integrity.

"So you shall tell my father of all my glory in Egypt, and of all that you have seen; and you shall hurry and bring my father down here" (Gen. 45:13).

After Joseph's dream came to pass, he became the prime minister of Egypt. He became wealthy and very comfortable because he was the number two man in the most powerful nation in the then world. When he met his brothers after thirteen years, he told them to notify their father of all his glory (wealth) in Egypt.

Most of the time we see glory as something too spiritual, like a white puffy cloud or a pillar of fire, but that is just one dimension of the meaning of the word "glory." Money, fame, cars, houses, and every good thing of life that God has made available for you to fulfill your divine purpose is described as glory. It is His desire to supply you with this glory more than you can ever fathom so that you can be a blessing to your world.

"Abram was very rich in livestock, in silver, and in gold" (Gen. 13:2).

"And you shall remember the LORD your God, for it is He who gives you power to get wealth, that He may establish His covenant which He swore to your fathers, as it is this day" (Deuteronomy 8:18).

We sing Abraham's "blessings are mine" because the man was rich in cattle, silver, and in gold. Some have a false opinion that too much wealth can lead one to hell. The question is, "Where is Abraham today after he enjoyed all his wealth while on earth?" In heaven, of course. As long as your wealth doesn't have you, you are on course. So anytime you make some money, just know that it is God that has given you the power to get it. If you are a serious minded Christian, tithing or giving generously to the cause of the kingdom, should never bring any hiccup, since you know it is God who gave you the power to be wealthy. We need to stop giving God leftovers, and start giving generously.

YOUR CORE COMPETENCE AND FINANCIAL SUCCESS

Financial success is not a mystery. It is too simple to be true. The good things of life will only gravitate towards the people who are adding values to humanity. People become blessed and financially prosperous to the degree of their value to the market place. The global economy is structured on this simple premise. The more valuable you are, the richer you become.

When you bring products or services that are valuable to people to the market place, you get rewarded in the process. Usually these products or services are closely linked with your dominant gifts. For example, if you are told to bring whatever you sell to a powerful man of God to anoint, so that God can prosper it, what will you bring? That's a million dollar question.

If somebody decides to bring a typewriter, because that is what he thinks is in vogue, and they pray fervently on it, that could be a wasted prayer, because only few people still buy typewriters in a twenty-first century digital age. Our prayer must be redefined in the light of the Scriptures. Effective prayer is not a one-size-fits-all, fire brigade, spiritual exercise. Prayer must be on target, specific, and scripturally relevant to your gift and purpose in life. If a person is not bringing any relevant value to the market place, prayer alone without a corresponding action will not be efficient as far as financial success is concerned. As long as we all use computers, Bill Gates will continually become wealthier. Mark Zuckerberg will always be rich as long as people are connected on Facebook all over the world.

As long as everyone uses Google search engine, Larry Page and others will continually make more money. In this era of technological advancement, nobody with their right mind will open a store that sells black and white televisions. The crux of the matter is, you do not become wealthy until you start adding relevant value to the lives of people by constantly and intentionally working your core gift.

Our prayer must be redefined in the light of the Scriptures. Effective prayer is not a one-size-fits-all, fire brigade, spiritual exercise. Prayer must be on target, specific, and scripturally relevant to your gift and purpose in life.

Become more organized and more business conscious with your gift. Apart from having a good knowledge of your divine purpose and dominant gift, you need to structure your life and package your gift neatly because people will only connect with you when you exhibit excellence in your area of specialty.

Study Guide

---

1. Meditation on God's word and activating your core gift is an ongoing process:
   a. How frequently do you do this? ___
   b. Where do you do it more effectively?
   c. What time of the day is best for you?
   d. What are your plans to do more of these activities?

2. What is your perception of money (financial blessing)?
   a. bad
   b. good
   c. neutral

3. Study and mediate with a group of friends (1 Tim. 4:13 and Deut. 8:18). Discuss their similarities.

4. Everything you'll ever need to fulfill your life assignment is wrapped up in your core gifts. Discuss this with a group using Bible and real life examples.

5. The sharper and more refined your core gift, the more value you bring to the market and the more profit you acquire. Which of your gifts are you currently working on?

Chapter 9

SYSTEMATIC TRANSITION STRATEGIES
Before You Fire Your Boss

FROM WHERE YOU ARE TO WHERE YOU SHOULD BE

This part of the book is so strategic and crucial because it could make all the difference in the world between identifying your purpose and its actual, practical fulfillment. Everybody is supposed to transition into their main, God-given purpose in life through their core, dominant gift. Most great people and successful people, especially those who are multi-gifted or multi-talented, will at a point have to get involved with jobs, occupations and other things that may look irrelevant to their gift or purpose in life. The truth is that they are all part of God's strategies to prepare them for their thrones.

Everything you have done so far and that you may currently be doing that might look like a waste of time could be part of God's program to transition you into His original purpose for your life.

"And we know that all things work together for good to those who love God, to those who are the called according to His purpose" (Romans 8:28).

Transition is a movement, passage, or change from one

> *Every major character that was used of God in the Bible had to go through the transition process which is always very crucial. I believe that a lot of great, gifted, talented, and brilliant individuals ruin their destiny at this stage. Many don't make it pass this phase. This is the state where, because of lack of understanding of pro-active transition strategies, individuals commit purpose hara-kiri.*

position, state or stage. In this context, transition is a movement or passage from doing what you probably don't like into doing what you love to do. There is the job you do for a living and there is what you were born and wired to do. One of the best places to be in life is when the two of them become one. Your life goes to a whole new level when what you were born and designed to do is also responsible for your livelihood. Transition is the pivotal state of life where you start learning to do what you love while learning to love what you do.

It is the place between existing and living. It is the place between happiness and joy; between where you move from your job to your work and where you move from surviving into meaning.

Every major character that was used of God in the Bible had to go through the transition process which is always very crucial. I believe that a lot of great, gifted, talented, and brilliant individuals ruin their destiny at this stage. Many don't make it pass this phase. This is the state where, because of lack of understanding of pro-active transition strategies, individuals commit purpose hara-kiri.

Examples of Bible characters who transitioned effectively include:

Abraham: the founding father of the Jewish nation went through this process. From a worshipper of the elements into a worshipper of Yahweh and into purpose and abundance.

Jacob: went from working for Laban to being a part owner of the business and finally owning his business.

Joseph: went from seeing the vision of greatness, moving into the pit; then from the pit into slavery; and from slavery to the prison from where he went to the throne.

David: transitioned from being a shepherd boy, to anointing/ordination; to being an anointed musician; to the killing of Goliath and into the palace; back into the wilderness (running from cave to cave for his dear life); and finally to the throne.

Moses: went from being Pharaoh's heir apparent to the throne; to recognizing his identity as a covenant person; into a fugitive and a shepherd boy; then finally into being called to lead Israel out of slavery.

Our Lord Jesus Christ: went through the passage from an innocent, twelve-year-old student of God's word in the synagogue, into a carpenter's son, then into a carpenter Himself; and finally into the ministry as the Savior.

It should be noted that because the period of transition is critically crucial and sensitive, the process can be circuitous. You need to be well informed and equipped with strategic information that will help you galvanize your inner composure by the help of the Holy Spirit.

WHAT HAPPENS DURING TRANSITION PERIOD?

There are feelings, signs and emotions to watch for when you are moving to the next phase of your purpose. They could be positive and negative at the same time. A part of you is excited and saying, "I have greatness inside me;" this is God's voice. Then other times you feel overwhelmed and go into depression; this is the enemy's attack.

Some of those negative and positive emotions include:

Table 2

Negative	Positive
1. A feeling of emptiness.	1. A feeling of "I am loaded with grace."
2. A feeling of being overwhelmed with pressures.	2. A feeling of life and excitement.
3. A feeling of distraction, especially if you are multi-talented.	3. A feeling of focus.
4. A feeling of loneliness or being abandoned.	4. A feeling of being alone with God where He shows you things others may not see.
5. A feeling of poverty and hopelessness.	5. A feeling of "I have all things."

If you constantly experience the negative emotions without the positive ones, it becomes unhealthy, if left unchecked could lead to any or all the negative manifestations including anger, bitterness, jealousy, rebellion, anxiety or even clinical depression caused by anger turned inside. Instead of experiencing an explosion of your God-given grace, you experience an implosion due to all the energy turned inward which is not healthy.

TIPS FOR SYSTEMATIC TRANSITION STRATEGY

It is vitally imperative to learn how to counter attack any negative emotion usually associated with transition. Learn to respond instead of react. There are usually two primary choices in life when you are faced with crisis. You can choose to accept the conditions as they exist or accept the responsibility for changing them.

Therefore, you can respond the following way:

1. Be diligent with whatever you are currently doing, *"And whatever you do, do it heartily, as to the Lord and not to men"* (Colossians 3:29). *"And if you have not been faithful in what is another man's, who will give you what is your own?"* (Luke 16:12). Learn from Joseph who in spite of his vision of becoming a prime minister served Potiphar diligently.

2. Be honest and faithful in your present level of assignment or vocation. God rewards faithfulness.

3. Surround yourself with positive people, like dream listeners, dream encouragers, dream interpreters, and dream makers. Negative people will drain your energy and demoralize your vision.

4. Invest in your future by buying books, CDs, and DVDs that are relevant to your core values in life. Your investment in this book is a sign that you mean business. Do not be a time spender, but a time investor. Use your spare time to work on yourself after getting off from your regular job. Identifying or recognizing your dominant gift is not enough, you must be effective, productive, and efficient with it. You've got to be intentional and deliberate in developing it by doing target practice which is a systematic, intentional, consistent, development and deployment of your gift.

I believe David used his spare time while the sheep grazed in the wilderness to sharpen his skills and gift of throwing rocks. If you are a writer, you can use your break time to write a blog or an article. If your passion is to own a restaurant, enroll in a part-time culinary school course. If your dominant gift is acting, singing or dancing, practice and rehearse everywhere. Instead of getting angry while in traffic, sing. Instead of engaging in gossip, dance. If your dominant gift has anything to do with speaking in public, read, study, and listen to good speakers.

5. Learn relationship tips and master them. Learn how to overcome low self-esteem, anger and other esteem problems through God's grace. The key point is: you have to be intentional which may mean cutting down on the time you spend on frivolities like watching TV and movies all day long. The brutal truth is: the people you are watching have mastered the gifts they are serving you with, that's why you are watching them. The question is: when will you start serving yours?

6. Do not burn the bridges behind you with your former employer or organization. No matter how bad the situation may appear, there will always be something to be proud of in that relationship. At some point, you might still need each other. In any case, that company, organization, ministry or boss, as the case may be, must have contributed one way or another to your life. You cannot re-write history. Honor them.

7. Write down and think on how you would want to be remembered when your time is up on earth. What do you want on your tombstone? What will you like people to remember about you, and more importantly what would God say about you? If what you are doing now is not what you want as your epitaph, then start a journey to what you want and what you want God to say at the end of your journey.

8. Have a consistent, grateful heart. No matter where you are in life, there are always reasons to be grateful to God more than complaints, grumblings, or murmurings. Be grateful for your spouse, children, career, house, your present job, etc. A heart of praise and thanksgiving has the capacity to activate and explode your faith for the next level in your transitional journey.

ADDITIONAL PRACTICAL TIPS FOR EFFECTIVE TRANSITION

1. Do a strategic mapping and analysis of your destiny by taking into practical consideration the 4W(s) and the H of purpose.

   What exactly is your God-given purpose in life?

   What core gift are you going to deploy for the fulfillment of that purpose?

   When do you want to start?

   Where is the geographical location and with whom do you want to do it?

   How do you want to do it?

   In other words, be accurately informed. Have all the available fundamental facts before embarking on the journey.

2. Check out the different ways of doing what you intend to do. Search and identify other options. For instance, if you want to start a food business, it is your responsibility to ascertain the model you want to explore. Is it fast food, franchise system, or independently owned.

3. Ask questions from people who honestly love and appreciate you. They could help you see your strength and blind spots. Most of the times we are emotionally attached to our babies (visions) to a point of ignoring reality checks that neutral people who genuinely love us can see.

4. Be flexible with choices and decisions that are not fundamentally etched in stones. For instance, fussing over whether to open your business to the public at 8 a.m. or 10 a.m. should not create a stalemate in your decision. Just simply go for the appropriate time that works for your customers. Do not attempt to make a permanent decision over a transient, ephemeral one.

5. Transitioning into your life's purpose through your core intelligence could be laborious. It may not always be a bed of roses but it is always worth it. After all, that is the essence of your life. Therefore, you should always examine the consequences and be pro-active.

6. Develop strategies to maximize your time. Effective transition involves a lot of time. You have to learn the skill of being able to stay

in touch with people and still be effective with time management at the same time. For me, I now prefer emails and texts. I only make phone calls when necessary. This will help you maintain your cutting-edge. The honest truth is, the more successful you become, the more people want to relate with you. It's a good thing and you should appreciate them for that, but you also need to put your life in order.

If the Return On Investment (ROI) is not greater than the effort, then the endeavor is not worth your time.

ROI is not all about the money. In this context, it includes intangible assets like character, insights, grace, and other things that money cannot buy. For example, thirty minutes with your

Do not waste your time on anything that is not profitable to your life's purpose. Young David will not fight where there are no spoils (rewards). "What shall be done to the man that kills the Philistine..." he asked (1 Samuel 17:26). If there is no profit, don't fight.

mentor could resolve a seven year old crisis. Essentially the point is: do not waste your time on anything that is not profitable to your life's purpose. Young David will not fight where there are no spoils (rewards). *"What shall be done to the man that kills the Philistine..."* he asked (1 Samuel 17:26). If there is no profit, don't fight.

Study Guide

___

1. Write down the gift that stands out the most every time you solve a problem.

2. What ability or gift do people refer to most in their relationship with you?

3. When your friends or loved ones call on you for assistance of any kind whether it is advice or opinion, what is the most recurrent topic?

4. If you were a salesperson, what would you sell without fail?

5. What is your present emotional state?
    a. Happy with what you are currently doing?
    b. Averagely satisfied?
    c. Unhappy?
    d. Extremely sad?
        If c) or d), what are your three pro-active exit strategies?
    a.
    b.
    c.

6. If you were debt free today and didn't have to pay any bills for the rest of your life, what would you be doing?

Part Three

UNMASKING THE REAL YOU

Chapter 10

SEARCHING FOR A NEEDLE IN A HAYSTACK

Creative Branding System for Effective Transition

The world is fast changing and the game changers of the last days need to wake up. In the arena of technology for example, Ray Leurzweil in his essay, "The law of Acceleration Returns," says that technology could not experience one hundred years of progress in the Twenty-first Century, it will be more like 20,000 years of progress at today's rate. In knowledge: by 1900, it had taken 150 years to double all human knowledge, today it takes only two years and by 2020, knowledge will double every seventy-two days according to estimates.

These challenges pose a threat for leaders who want to maintain the status quo. To be relevant, you can't afford to not be on the cutting edge of whatever is your calling in life and develop the skills to navigate through the turbulent water of aggressive globalization and competition.

Darren Hardy, in his editorial of *Success Magazine*, April 2011 edition, corroborates my point: "...today the speed of change demands a completely different leader: one who can rapidly adapt to change, requiring constant involvement in skill development. They will need to be expert in human capital, not just financial capital, master emotional intelligence, not just economic competence, not just control but align people through meaning and purpose..." All I am saying is: you need to uniquely stand out in your calling in life. It is called branding.

The word "branding" is used in many conversations, but the fact is, very few people actually know what it really entails. According to Webster dictionary, "branding is a variety of something distinguished by some distinctive characteristics." Though its process can be involving, its goal is simple; the creation and development of a specific identity for a product, group or person that marks him or her out from the crowd.

In the context of this message, it is carefully and creatively designed to present qualities that your Creator had in mind while creating you with the purpose of being a blessing to your world and it is meant to be developed and carried on for the long haul. Maybe you are highly gifted and very knowledgeable about several things but still cannot find your bearing because your societal impact is not commensurate with your giftedness and abilities.

Jesus said:

"(18)The Spirit of the LORD is upon Me, because He has anointed Me to preach the gospel to the poor; He has sent Me to heal the brokenhearted, to proclaim liberty to the captives and recovery of sight to the blind, to set at liberty those who are oppressed (19)To proclaim the acceptable year of the LORD" (Luke 4:18-19).

According to the Scripture above, Jesus Christ was not confused with His various gifts but focused on the main ministry of preaching the good news. He was a very strategic Person, He directed all His abilities to the fulfillment of that main purpose. He was not confused but focused all his energy on His brand.

"He who sins is of the devil, for the devil has sinned from the beginning. For this purpose the Son of God was manifested, that He might destroy the works of the devil" (1 John 3:8).

While Jesus was busy going about His business on earth, He cast out demons from people, opened the eyes of the blind, and fed the hungry to mention a few. He used His gifts to establish God's kingdom on earth. He cared so much for the people He ministered to. He was not only there to save their souls, but made sure they were well taken care of spiritually, materially, emotionally, and even mentally. Everything He did was to express that main purpose—establishing God's kingdom everywhere He went.

Your life should reflect the life of Jesus if you appropriately brand your gifts and talents. While fulfilling your purpose, effective personal branding will give you a specific identity that portrays you clearly in the mind of other people because you have resolved to stay true to the course of your destiny. It will help you avoid distraction which is one of the major temptations facing people that are multi-gifted.

PERSONAL BRANDING

A type of branding that is fast becoming more popular these days is personal branding. According to Dan Scwabel, author of *me 2.0*, "personal branding describes the process by which individuals and entrepreneurs differentiate themselves and stand out from a crowd by identifying and articulating their unique value proposition."

I believe this uniqueness must be accompanied with authenticity and integrity. You must consistently endeavor to build a good reputation or else people will not take you seriously. Also, your brand must be very clear, unambiguous and uncluttered.

Maintain simplicity and avoid cumbersomeness that could project you as complex. Laura Cross of *rock your expertise inc.* says "A brand is the powerful, clear, positive, idea that comes to mind whenever other people think of you." In other words, what are your values, creativities, and visions?

To develop a sustainable, creative brand, you've got to include components of who you are as a person, your core service or product, your uniqueness, and what differentiates you from your competitors. An effective branding includes creating a peculiar, distinctive model that is uncommon. In the marketing world it is called your Unique Selling Proposition (USP). When your name is mentioned, what image or vision is presented in the minds of the people, potential audience or buyer? For instance, the image of faith in God's word, the blessing and integrity comes to mind anytime names like Rev. Kenneth Copeland and Dr. Creflo Dollar are mentioned. Dr. Myles Munroe projects purpose, Pastor Benny Hinn is healing, Pastor Enoch Adeboye is holiness and miracles, while Dr. John Maxwell is leadership to mention a few names.

Branding experts always advice that you build your brand around a smaller, narrower defined market within your global niche. It is believed that the more specific, smaller target market you have, the better your chances of success. The honest truth is that you are not sent to help everybody in the world. If only one person could solve everybody's problems, then the rest of the human race would be useless. So when you target a particular market or audience with your personal brand, you will stand out and attract that market base.

Even the educational sector understands the basic elements of specialty in various fields of study. The narrower you become in your chosen profession, which is likely already crowded, the better you become and the more people you will attract. For example, there are medical doctors but there are also pediatricians who specialize in certain diseases affecting children.

There are lawyers who handle just about any case but there are those who deal with specific issues like insurance, domestic abuse, civil cases, etc. You've got to be specific. Anyone who wants to be known for everything will eventually be known for nothing. If you want to be a jack of all trades, that's fine, but please be a master of one. Your audience or client cannot afford to be confused with your identity. Your particular identity and consistency will create a true ownership of your brand and make you an expert in your field. When you consistently and actively work on your expertise, you are most likely going to achieve the following:

- You will become better in your expertise and brand. Repetitions will make you better.

- You are likely going to have a better following of clients or those who need what you have. People will always follow or listen to people who they believe are the best in what they do. Kentucky Fried Chicken (KFC) cannot do a better job than Coca Cola when it comes to soda neither can Coca Cola outdo McDonald's with fries.

- You will become the go-to expert that people can refer to thereby making you an expert that could command higher fees for whatever you offer.

Ability to clearly identify your market niche through a creative, systematic branding and an articulate presentation of your life changing expertise will go a long way in establishing your success.

Having a personal, creative branding solution is the wave of the future because it creates visibility which allows you to contagiously transfer or spread your influence to others. If you are perceived as an expert in your career or calling, you will win in the competitive global marketplace.

Perception as one of the key elements of creative personal branding is always being examined by smart organizations because if perception is negative, no matter how valuable your product or service is, you may not go far. The story of a rich woman who took care of the man of God in 2 Kings Chapter 4:9 is contextually relevant here. She and her husband built a penthouse for

> *Having a personal, creative branding solution is the wave of the future because it creates visibility which allows you to contagiously transfer or spread your influence to others.*
> *If you are perceived as an expert in your career or calling, you will win in the competitive global marketplace.*

the man of God and made sure he was always comfortable because she said *"I perceive that this is a holy man of God, who passes by us regularly."* Positive perception of Billy Graham based on God's grace and positive track records injects hope in people as they make their way to the altar to commit their life to God as the choir sings the trademark song, "Just As I Am..."

Effective, consistent personal brand built on integrity makes success predictable. The way you want to be perceived is imperative. Please understand that because of the desire of every human to live in freedom including that of speech, people will label you according to their perception. You have probably even been perceived as a hard worker, workaholic, passionate, lazy, arrogant, brilliant, etc.

You see, your personal brand has failed if people's perception of you is at variance with your life's vision. Your personal brand must line up with your core values and identity. If it is the other way around, then there is identity crisis here. It is your responsibility through God's word and a consistent desire on your part to develop corresponding character traits that will counter any negative perception. For instance, if you are being perceived as an arrogant, rebellious person, learn to be more respectful. If people think you are lazy, be more productive because if you don't define yourself, people will do it for you. Studies show that it only takes thirty seconds for people to form a lasting impression of you and more than eighteen interactions to change their minds if the first impression was negative.

Now, I am not by any means implying that you should live your life in bondage trying to please everybody. What I do mean is as much as possible within the grace that God has given you, follow peace and integrity with all men. In the final analysis, you cannot seek the approval of men to live. Joyce Meyer, in her book *Approval Addiction Syndrome*, has a lot of powerful nuggets that could help.

BENEFITS OF BRANDING

Personal branding will help you focus more on your principal gift. There will be occasions in your life when you are tempted to stretch yourself too thin in order to achieve many things. This only comes with a price of neglecting other important things in your life, such as spending less time with your spouse or children which could lead to a dysfunctional family.

Branding helps you to be emotionally connected to those who need you. When you are properly branded, people bond with you by their mere thoughts of you because you have distinguished yourself as an expert in a particular area of endeavor. This gives you credibility because you have earned their trust. Credibility will lead to loyalty and loyalty will lead to profitability.

For instance, Coca-Cola as a brand is the most popular and biggest-selling soft drink in history, as well as the best known product in the world. Over the years people have trusted its manufacturer and the product itself. Coca-Cola is now a multi-million dollar business.

Coke is just a mixture of a few ingredients, but its proper branding has increased and transformed it into a household name. It is highly necessary to become an expert in whatever you are called to do or wired for because the world is becoming more competitive. The technological advancements taking place all over the world reveal that it is not enough for you to know what to do; but you must go to the next level of branding yourself. Some companies are worth millions of dollars today just because they are in the business of branding. In the fashion industry, corporations like Ralph Lauren, T. M. Lewin, Levis Strauss, Tommy Hilfiger, and Thomas Pink to mention a few, have made fortunes because their brand names have set them apart.

The automobile industry is no different; cars like Toyota, Volvo, Honda, Mercedes Benz, BMW, Volkswagen and Rolls Royce have been in vogue so far. These cars are being sold daily even when there is economic crisis because of their identity. There is no level of promotion that can convince some people to buy a BMW; all because they are emotionally connected to a particular brand name called Mercedes and vice-versa.

Some close friends of mine have more than three different types of Mercedes Benz cars. Mercedes Benz came up with an advertisement slogan some years ago which says "there are only two cars in the world: Mercedes Benz and others." BMW or Toyota may not agree with them, but that's their brand cliché and it is working for them.

Also, there are many educational institutions in the world but some have carved out a name for themselves because of their reputation. Some people are proud to be graduates of Ivy League schools like Harvard, Cambridge, Yale, Princeton or Oxford. People who study at Yale, Cambridge, or Stanford think they have an advantage over others, which may be a subjective argument but that is what effective branding does.

Two years ago in the United States of America, the art and science of politics went to another level. Many in the nation came out en masse to vote, some waited for three or four hours to cast their votes, many for the very first time in their lives because they believed that this time must be different and their vote could be that difference. This was only possible because political strategists discovered a suitable candidate who they could brand effectively for the highest office in the country. The branding consultants assembled the best campaign team ever in the history of politics around the then Senator Barack Obama because of his profound ability to communicate.

He was well advised and guided to center all his campaign speeches on the brand word, "Change." He did it so eloquently and the rest is history. Barack Obama may not be the most intelligent person in the Democratic Party but he became a rising star within the party in 2004, when he delivered a rousing speech at the Democratic National Convention.

The lesson from this is; you should endeavor to focus on your main competence by creatively branding your core gift. Harnessing the power of branding requires discipline, but it pays off in the end because it will single you out of the billions of people living in the world and will also make you authentic.

You can only be authentic in your purpose because you are fashioned for it. Branding your main gift that is most relevant to your divine mission on earth will make that possible for you. For your branding to advance to the next level, you need to be consistent with your image and the way it's being projected.

This is achievable when you focus on your distinct area of specialty, which is natural for you. Branding gives you clarity. If communication is your dominant gift, endeavor to speak your passion all the time whether you are invited for a special function or not. After actively engaging it for a long while, you will have clarity on the best way to excpress yourself.

> *You can only be authentic in your purpose because you are fashioned for it. Branding your main gift that is most relevant to your divine mission on earth will make that possible for you.*

THE TREE ANALYSIS OF PERSONAL BRANDING

The analysis of a tree will shed more light on the concept of branding. The parts of a tree are the roots, trunk(s), branches, fruits and leaves. Your physical body is the trunk while the root is that part of you which is usually unseen.

THE ROOT

It is your foundation and your unseen connection with God. When you exercise spiritually either by meditating or obeying God's word, praying, fasting, or worshipping with other believers in a church assembly, you are building your character. You develop the fruits of the spirit when you truthfully engage in those positive activities after an extensive period of time. Through those spiritual exercises, you are connecting with God, who nurtures you so that your roots can grow deeper. As your roots are being strengthened, the easy flow of nutrients in and out of them will boost your fruit output. The taller the building, the deeper the foundation must be.

Perhaps you have been laboring in the word for a long time. You have been fasting and praying on a consistent basis. You have been following the leading of the spirit, but it looks like nobody seems to recognize all you do and what you are going through right now. You are going through the process of building a strong foundation which enhances your connection with God.

God is working on you, purging away all the impurities in your life that could slow you down in pursuit of purpose. He wants you to be strong because He knows that in these last days, challenges of life will confront you to test how grounded you are in God. Some people will be blown away by these storms, but hold on tight to God because in Him you live, move and have your being. Billy Graham, in *The Storm Warning*, eschatologically encourages the church to hold on tight to the only hope of the world, Jesus Christ. Jesus says;

> *"(24) Therefore whoever hears these sayings of Mine, and does them, I will liken him to a wise man who built his house on the rock: (25) and the rain descended, the floods came, and the winds blew and beat on that house; and it did not fall, for it was founded on the rock (26) But everyone who hears these sayings of Mine, and does not do them, will be like a foolish man who built his house on the sand (27) and the rain descended, the floods came, and the winds blew and beat on that house; and it fell. And great was its fall"* (Matt. 7:24-27).

The difference between the two houses is their foundations. The test of time will show the authenticity of the building you are constructing, whether it is a house, your home or business empire. Whatever you are building, are you building it on a strong foundation? Make sure you are building properly because in the process, you are going to face some challenges. A lot of people want to bear fruits before they grow downwards. It doesn't happen that way.

Your seed is much akin to the growing process of the Chinese bamboo tree; it takes time. A time will come when you can't stop the inflow of success coming your way because of the seeds you have sown.

THE BRANCHES

Next to the roots are your branches. These are your gifts and talents. The branches within branches refer to your various abilities that spring out from the main trunk. Fruits are the ultimate goal of a tree, but a tree without branches cannot bear fruits.

THE FRUITS

The fruit of the tree is your purpose. Jesus told His disciples, *"...but I chose you and appointed you that you should go and bear fruit, and that your fruit should remain"* (John 15:16). What kind of fruits are you bearing? There is no use of a tree that is not bearing fruits. In view of this, Jesus cursed the fig tree in Mark 11 because it was not fulfilling its reason for existence. Your purpose in life is the fruit you should bear, which in turn bears more fruits as you become more engaged in it.

The fruits represent the products or results of your brand and expertise because they have come to stay.

THE LEAVES

Leaves beautify the tree. People come around under the shadow of a tree to rest. Nobody hides under the shadow of a leafless tree. The leaves are the physical manifestations of the blessings of God in your life such as cars, houses, money and other material blessings. These will automatically flow in your direction as you sharpen your dominant gifts to fulfill your purpose.

Naturally, the leaves of a tree can wither in some seasons. But you as a blessed saint of God are like a tree that brings forth its fruit in its season, and whose leaves also shall not wither provided you abide continually in God and His word.

"[1]Blessed is the man who walks not in the counsel of the ungodly, nor stands in the path of sinners, nor sits in the seat of the scornful [2]But his delight is in the law of the LORD, and in His law he meditates day and night [3]He shall be like a tree planted by the rivers of water, that brings forth its fruit in its season, whose leaf also shall not wither; and whatever he does shall prosper" (Ps. 1:1-3).

Abiding in God's word by meditating on it regularly keeps you connected with God with your roots firmly attached to Him. You also develop roots when you are fully engaged in the things of God.

"(12)The righteous shall flourish like a palm tree, he shall grow like a cedar in Lebanon (13)Those who are planted in the house of the LORD shall flourish in the courts of our God (14)They shall still bear fruit in old age; they shall be fresh and flourishing" (Ps. 92:12-14).

Every part of the palm tree is useful. Believers walking along the path of their purpose will still be bearing fruits until they die. This is why your foundation has to be very firm so that you will not be distracted by the issues of life. In the course of fulfilling your purpose, you are bound to prosper in everything you do.

God cannot fail in any of His undertakings and He is working through you on earth, therefore you cannot fail if you are fulfilling His program for you. The blessing of God empowers you to be wealthy without sorrow. When God blesses you, the blessings remain in and with you. People only know about you after you have branded yourself, by developing and nurturing your dominant gift to a fruitful stage. This is the mysterious stage in life in which everything you do prospers.

Study Guide

---

1. Discuss with a group of your friends three reasons why they should do a personal branding of their core gifts.

2. Write three negative consequences of ignoring the advice on branding.

    a.

    b.

    c.

3. What will your vision statement in life read?

4. What will your mission statement read?

5. Identify five demographics of your audience or clients.

    a.

    b.

    c.

    d.

    e.

6. Write down three main reasons why you think they should listen to you or do business with you.

7. Identify and write down four distractions of your unique brand and proffer solutions on how to practically eliminate them.

    a.

    b.

    c.

    d.

Chapter 11

RECESSION IS A MYTH

The Wealthy Poor

While ministering in our local church on a Sunday morning, I asked the people if they could each raise 20,000 dollars within a month. Majority of them said they could never get such an amount in such a short time frame. Some said they would make an effort but would give up if it looked like they were going to fail. Then I illustrated to them that, assuming I'm a friend of a very wealthy man who tells me, "Sam, I really want to be a blessing to some people, however, they will have to make a commitment of 20,000 dollars to register for training in Washington D.C. on how to be a world class investor and on how I became a billionaire.

"The first twenty people who enroll for this seminar will be loaned ten million dollars each, to be paid back in the next five years with only 2 percent interest." After mentioning this hypothetical, lifetime opportunity, a great number of them answered affirmatively that they would raise the funds. The truth is, there is no shortage of money. People purchase what they think is important to them based on perception, which can be subjective.

In fact, it has been said that if it were possible to take all the millions and billions of dollars from those who have them and give them to the poor so the rich become poor and vice-versa, studies show that in just a matter of a few years, those millions and billions would make their way back into the hands of those who had them in the first place and the poor would become broke again. Why? It is all about perception and mindset. Real wealth is intangible. The one that cannot be seen is the real asset. In Genesis 25:5-6, Abraham gave gifts (the tangible) to Ishmael but *all* he had, the *blessing* (the intangible), to Isaac. Ability to access the blessing (intangible) makes for unlimited financial resources.

The title of this chapter is an oxymoron that explains the complexity of the psychology of poverty and riches. In this chapter, through God's word and relatable human experiences, we will see that recession is not real. It is a myth. It is only real to those who have accepted the status-quo. It is all about perception. You have to be able to do that mental transition into the truth that could demystify recession.

It is imperative that we establish a fundamental fact about the supernatural provision God has made available for you to fulfill your purpose. Everything that you'll ever need to do what He has called you to do, no matter how gigantic it may appear, has been provided for in Christ Jesus. As established earlier, every dime, million, or billion, as the case may be, that would be required to finish it has been made available.

"...*For all things are yours*" (1 Corinthians 3:21).

Each time you pray to God for anything in the name of Jesus Christ by faith, the answer leaves the throne room that moment, but the manifestation is usually in the hands of a person or group of people. Even when God releases angelic assistance, they will still go through human beings most of the time. Remember the story of Cornelius in Acts 10? Cornelius still had to connect with Peter physically to receive the desired result.

As long as there are human beings on the earth, what God has given you will always be relevant. Paul, the Jewish Apostle encourages young Timothy to develop and deploy his gift so that he could become profitable;

"*[13]Till I come, give attention to reading, to exhortation, to doctrine. [14]Do not neglect the gift that is in you, which was given to you by prophecy with the laying on of the hands of the eldership. [15]Meditate on these things; give yourself entirely to them, that your progress may be evident to all*" (1 Tim. 4:13-15).

The Greek etymology of the word "gift" is interesting; it is *Charis*, from where Charisma is derived, which means "divine gratuity, favor, grace, endowment, free gift and miraculous faculty."

Essentially, charisma or gift is God's divine enablement and unmerited favor. It has nothing to do with your level of education, the color of your skin, background, gender or social class.

It is also amazing to know that the Greek word for "stir" in the passage means to "rekindle, to sharpen, to refine, to re-fire, to engage, to develop, to activate, to put pressure upon or to be productive, efficient, and effective." While to profit means "to have dividends, gains, positive results, abundance, peace, prosperity and God's goodness." All these will be the physical realities of an engaged gift.

From the foregoing, it is clear that your gift will attract the good things of life if properly channeled. The caveat though is that even though God has blessed humanity with every

Some of the poorest people on earth are very nice. It took me a long time to understand this. If you have nothing valuable to offer, you will soon be deserted. That is life.

good thing that would make life comfortable, those good things like riches and abundance will only gravitate or move in the direction of those who are adding values with their God-given endowments. The honest truth is, people become financially prosperous to the degree of the values they bring to the market place. The global economy is run on this simple but profound concept. The more valuable you are through your God-given ability, the richer you become. Money or financial surplus does not come to you because you pray or fast, as good as these are. Money does not even go to nice people because they are nice. Some of the poorest people on earth are very nice. It took me a long time to understand this. If you have nothing valuable to offer, you will soon be deserted. That is life.

However, if you bring products or services that are indispensably valuable to the market place, you'll get rewarded in the process. That is the way the universe is structured to operate. The life-changing truth is, most of the spiritual activities like praying in tongues, fasting, and demon binding will still have to translate to their physical realities that are consumable or usable in the real world before you get rewarded.

For example, how many people today will want to buy typewriters or radiogram? (Some younger generation may not even know what a radiogram is). Imagine a Christian brother fasting and praying for forty days to sell these items. He means well but he is not offering what is needed for consumers in the twenty-first century; he is living in the past.

The size of the problem you are solving sometimes determines the size and the quality of the rewards you get. The level of material prosperity you experience is most of the time proportionate to the service or product you offer. The only exception is the grace of God on your gift that gives more than what you are worth naturally, yet even with that you still need to bring value to the table. Furthermore, it has been said that when "opportunity meets preparation, explosive success is inevitable." You've got to constantly be updating yourself in the acquisition of relevant skills to meet up with changing times. I completely agree with Abraham Lincoln who said "the dogmas of the quiet past are inadequate to the stormy present."

What is happening economically in the world today is a historic, global convergence of unusual opportunities and open doors for those who can make that spiritual and intelligent transition to see those unique doors. No one person is immutable, we all need one another.

Money is a liquid that flows in the direction of those who have something to offer. Other people's crises are other people's opportunities. That is the way the global economy is meant to function. Everyone is supposed to pay for their ignorance in one way or another and everyone is supposed to receive certain financial rewards for their expertise. For example, if everybody knew how to fix their cars, mechanics would be broke. People's health crises are a competent doctor's opportunity. Other people's legal challenges are a good lawyer's delight. If everyone were always happy, comedians, singers, and other people in the entertainment industry would be unnecessary. As long as there are people with family issues or those who want to know God at a higher level existing in this world, genuine ministers, counselors and therapists will forever be relevant.

Therefore, what is happening today in the economy that is commonly referred to as recession, is simply a perfect storm for creative, pro-active, deliberate, value-adding covenant minded individuals.

Therefore, what is happening today in the economy that is commonly referred to as recession, is simply a perfect storm for creative, pro-active, deliberate, value-adding covenant minded individuals. Historically, recessions come and they go. It happened many times in the Bible. Abraham went through famine (recession); Isaac did and so did Jacob and Joseph, but they all conquered it. So recession is not new. What you do with it is more important than recession itself.

Interestingly, about sixteen of the DOW companies were started during past recessions. They include the famous McDonald's, Procter & Gamble, Johnson and Johnson, Disney, and General Electric. This global challenge is simply creating rooms for the new kings of the kingdom to be crowned within the next few months or years, depending on your readiness and faith level.

The current, economic imbroglio has created new problems waiting for the Davids and the Josephs of our generation to solve and get rewarded in the process. The playing field has been leveled. The so called poor of this generation no longer have excuses because for the first time in human history, both the rich and the poor have access to the same information through the internet. You see, opportunities exist everywhere as long as your ultimate purpose is to add value. Do not chase money but seek to solve people's problems, then money will chase you. Money is everywhere but most people can't see it.

Read the following amazing statistics. They will help you agree with me that recession indeed is a MYTH:

40 percent of the world's wealth is in the United States (even as "broke" as some fear-mongering experts may want us to believe).

40 percent of the wealth in the United States is in the hands of one percent of the population

It further states that if all the money in the U.S. were to be taken over by the government and redistributed equally so that the U.S. becomes a socialist republic (which I don't pray for), everybody on U.S. soil today, including children, would have three million dollars each. Now that's powerful. What that tells you is that the minimum you should aspire to have in your lifetime is three million dollars. Your money is probably in the hands of somebody who may be adding value somewhere. These staggering statistics are just for the United States alone, how much more when you become global in your approach to solving problems.

Sometime ago, I tried to narrow this revelation down to my beautiful state of Maryland, USA where I live with my family. The population here is about six million people. Think about this:

1. Almost six million people eat different types of food.
2. Over five million people sleep on beds and they need mattresses, sheets, and pillows.
3. Let's say over one million would need at least one car.
4. They will put gas in those cars.
5. They will need to service or tune-up their cars.
6. A couple of million of them will want to get married and buy wedding gowns, suits, shoes, and have wedding receptions.
7. Over five million would drink some kind of water or juice every day.
8. Their children go to school and will need school supplies.

The list goes on. The needs are just too many. But the big question begging for a desperate answer is how many of these problems are "prayerful Christians" solving effectively? One of the excuses many people give is "would people be able to afford my product, wouldn't they say it is overpriced?" This is another myth. "Nothing is expensive or unaffordable." "This is too expensive" is relative. It depends on the value or the need. You see, the real problem with many people is that they have a consumer mentality syndrome. They need to flip that mentality around and become producers.

In the so called economic depression, millions of people all over the world are still paying to go watch their favorite teams play, see movies at the theaters and other entertaining interests.

The point is: people buy whatever they think is important to them, based on their perception. Your perception is a product of your thought patterns. That's why the word of God says;

"For as he thinks in his heart, so is he..." (Prov. 23:7).

The universal law of seed time and harvest would always propel certain things to produce the physical, material equivalent of your thoughts. Whatever dominates your thought will always move in your direction.

Study these principles on thought and perception:

1. Whatever you think and focus on will always automatically expand. So, imagine you focus on your dominant gift to serve your generation.

2. Your thoughts produce your feelings, your feelings produce your words, your words produce your decisions, your decisions produce your actions, your actions produce your habits and your habits produce your destiny.

3. Your subconscious mind is much more active and powerful than your conscious mind. This is a blessing, but also dangerous because of its neutrality. Your subconscious mind does not have the capacity to know the difference between a truth and a lie, a curse and a blessing, except you renew your mind daily with God's word.

It receives and processes whatever information is fed with until whatever is stored begins to produce its physical reality. Read this powerful scripture.

"Jesus said to him, 'If you can believe, all things are possible to him who believes" (Mark 9:23).

Even though, Jesus made this statement in the context of us receiving the good provisions made available to us, I believe the opposite is also true.

POINTS TO NOTE

1. Develop your gift to a point that if people have to pay huge sums of money for you to serve them your service or product, they would not feel the impact of the cost because of their perception that the value they are receiving is far greater than the price. It will be a win-win situation. That is the way I feel after reading a book or watching a movie I really like. The so-called high-end price does not really matter anymore.

2. Because your God-given gift is recession-proof, it would conquer and soar high in any economy as long as it is backed by heaven. Some Bible scholars believe that the reason God did not ask Noah to add fishes to the list of creatures to be put in the ark before the flood was because fishes will survive and conquer the flood. Your God-given gift should find its best and highest expression during crisis period. In fact, that is one of the proofs it is from God.

3. You can never be poor because there is no shortage in God's kingdom as long as you serve your gift efficiently and effectively.

4. It is highly important for you to know that there was not a single person that God made rich or wealthy in the Bible who had nothing to bring to the table. They were not just prosperous because they were God's people, they were prosperous because God was with them and blessed the works of their hands and whatever they brought to the table that was valuable. I cannot over-emphasize this point because a lot of Christians are stuck here because somebody went to the extreme by telling them that riches will come if they can pray, fast, bind demons, give tithes and offerings without adding the importance of real life, market transaction principles. Any attempt to suggest that money would move into the hands of anybody not offering valuable, relevant service or product is illegal. It is called stealing and people go to jail for that reason. However, certain types of imprisonments are not physical. It could be financial, emotional, psychological or even spiritual imprisonment as a result of mental or spiritual laziness. The result is that, in the body of Christ is a whole bunch of embittered, frustrated, angry Christians who think they are being raped or manipulated because they don't seem to be getting results. I believe one of the main kernels of this book is to fill this gap without also going to the other extreme of neglecting the place of God's grace.

The honest truth staring all of us in the face today is the fact that some of the major conglomerates representing different industries like food, automobile, technology, telecommunications etc. are being run successfully using real life principles of exchanging products or services for money. In fact, many prayerful, Holy Spirit filled Christians work for these companies.

Let's look at some Bible characters that became successful because of God's grace and their value systems.

1. Jacob, who has been labeled a thief by many preachers in my opinion, did not actually steal Esau's birthright because he bought it. There was an exchange. Jacob brought a delicious food (product) to the table and Esau bought it with his birthright and even signed a legal document (an oath in those days was equivalent to a legal document today). I think it was Esau who was trying to steal by trying to claim back what he already sold legally. You cannot eat your cake and have it at the same time. Jacob couldn't have been a thief. Have you ever thought for a moment that God would ever bless and prosper a thief and even identify with him to the point of even changing and immortalizing his name till today? Jacob knew the importance of bringing values to the table so well that he used the same principle for Laban (a type of worldly system—wicked, cheat, greedy etc.). Jacob brought his witty invention to the table and asked for part equity ownership of Laban's business before he finally started his own.

2. David's valuable service that was responsible for his wealth and success was his strategic warfare expertise or military might.

3. Solomon was always bringing wisdom to the table to resolve complex issues. That would be consulting in today's language. The point is, no one is entitled to any significant reward in life until they wake up to the reality of the way life is organized by the Creator: become valuable and become prosperous. Simple. This concept is explained into details in the chapter addressing the prophetic wealth transfer.

Study Guide

---

1. Write and discuss three reasons why you agree that recession is a myth and not real.

   a.

   b.

   c.

2. What is the valuable product or service you intend or are already bringing to the market place?

3. If you have a consumer mentality, how do you intend to transition into a producer mindset? Write and discuss with your accountability partners or study group the three strategies you want to employ.

4. Is your product or service tangible or intangible? If intangible, how do you quantify its worth?

5. Identify and write three reasons why you believe that your core gifts are recession proof.

   a.

   b.

   c.

6. What is your market?

7. Discuss the demography of your clients, audience, or consumers.

Chapter 12

RELATIONSHIP EQUITY

Building a Sustainable Platform

Everybody wants to be successful and there is nothing abnormal about that. Some not only yearn for success but desire generational success. As a result of this, parents encourage their children to study Medicine, Law, Journalism and other seemingly lucrative courses in school. Some parents even "force" their children to study what they (parents) couldn't. Most of these parents don't mean to be controlling, they just want the success flow to continue in their family. They may be using the wrong approach, but the goal is for their children to be successful. So success is a desire that God has put into every heart.

"This Book of the Law shall not depart from your mouth, but you shall meditate in it day and night, that you may observe to do according to all that is written in it. For then you will make your way prosperous, and then you will have good success" (Josh. 1:8).

Therefore, a desire for success is not a bad idea at all but we must understand its art and science from the lens of God's word. There are laws or principles governing the operation of everything in the universe including success. A constant, ignorant or deliberate violation of these laws, inherently have their negative repercussions packaged in them. For instance, if a person violates the law of gravity by jumping out of the window for any reason, he can hurt himself. That is almost automatic. The injury sustained in the process of the violation of the law is not caused by demons except the person is under their direct control.

In the same way, there are friendly universal laws God put in place to help guide us into our purpose. One of them is the law of magnet.

BUILDING A PLATFORM THROUGH THE LAW OF MAGNET

The law of magnet which some refer to as the law of attraction is like an impetus for building a successful platform. If you cannot offer any perceived value, no one will come near you. That's just life. Jesus recognized and believed His peculiar anointing, walked in it without stress, and was able to attract the people who appreciated it. When you are gifted for a particular task, you attract the people that the gift is meant for. Today's pastors ought to understand that the church is not meant for "dignified people." Neither is it meant for those who know how to love their wives or honor their husbands. We may come across people like that from time to time, but the anointing usually attracts raw people. The anointing is meant to attract people who don't know their way in life, those who are sick, and those who don't know how to relate with their spouses. The power of God, and His principles revealed in the Scriptures should fix them. The purpose of the anointing is to break yokes and remove burden from people.

> *It should be understood that success cannot be achieved in isolation, no matter who you are. Life is designed in such a way that human beings function effectively when they relate together in love especially to those with whom they are connected.*

It should be understood that success cannot be achieved in isolation, no matter who you are. Life is designed in such a way that human beings function effectively when they relate together in love especially to those with whom they are connected. There is no such thing as a "self-made person." Somebody must have contributed to your success one way or another, at some point.

The person that doesn't have healthy relationships is the real poor person. When the Bible encourages us to " love one another" (1 John 3:11), it is to our advantage because He knows that the majority of the resources that we will ever need to do what He has called us to do regardless of its enormous size is always tied to other human beings.

Of course, your motivation for loving people should not be based on what you can get but what you can give. When the Bible says that "it is more blessed to give than to receive," it simply means the more you give the more you receive.

If Jesus were to be physically here on earth today, you can imagine what His congregation would look like. You would probably see several lame, blind, rebellious and devious people who refuse to obey the instructions of the ushers. Would you like to sit beside people that look unkept in church?

Would you sit beside a person who has not had a bath for one month? When your pastor asks you to turn and greet your neighbor, would you like to turn to such a person? Would you put your hands around that person and hug them? The question is, could that person be connected to your destiny one way or the other? That is what the real church of Jesus is called to do; to love the unlovable. Building a platform for effective relationship is not only crucial but mandatory in the school of success. In fact, I believe this is probably the best equity or resources anybody has

The idea of burning bridges behind us and cutting off people because they don't agree with us is not only unscriptural but demonic. Another name for it is ARROGANCE. The truth is, the bridge you are trying to burn today may be the one that would connect you to your next level in the future.

apart from God. It is all about walking in love and looking for the best in other people. Anybody who will do well in any life endeavor must learn the skills required to relate with people. The idea of burning bridges behind us and cutting off people because they don't agree with us is not only unscriptural but demonic. Another name for it is ARROGANCE. The truth is, the bridge you are trying to burn today may be the one that would connect you to your next level in the future. Don't you think these statements are rather too strong? You may ask, I am glad you asked. Check the following observations and you would agree with me that the statements above may be absolute but they are true.

1. God loves everybody no matter who they are. Therefore, cutting off people or having bitterness against them will upset God.

2. People go through different seasons and changes. The person you are trying to avoid or cut off from may have grown or become more matured in the areas that were causing friction between you and him in the first place. So, how would you know if you don't ever want to see him again?

3. The person you don't want to have any dealings with today may be your lifeline tomorrow.
4. Relationship is not about what we can get, but about what we can give to the other person. The question is, what can you bring to the table to help this person?
5. Bitterness and resentment would hold you captive.

The Bible is filled with people who at one time had challenges with other people but in the end they worked out their differences. For instance, Paul and John Mark had a dispute in Acts 10: 36-39 and were separated for a while but later became friends again (Philemon 1:24).

Demas forsook Apostle Paul for the transient trappings of the mundane things of life but later became matured. Paul referred to him as a fellow laborer in Philemon 1:24. To fathers and mentors, the story of the prodigal son should be your guiding light. There was a temporary friction on that relationship but the father did not reject the son when he came back. He was not even asked to refund the money he squandered. I am not by any means recommending prodigality. I am only implying that there is no sin that is beyond forgiveness except blasphemy against the Holy Spirit.

The balance here is, certain toxic relationships that are constantly putting you down should be avoided. They include:

a. Those who tolerate you.
b. Those who constantly put you down.
c. Those who consistently criticize you and destroy you.
d. Those who are not going anywhere with their life.
e. Those who teach heresies or those who have completely departed from the faith.
f. Those who don't respect your time or privacy.

These are my recommendations for those who abuse certain privileges because of ignorance. Learning to respect people's time especially if that relationship is a privileged one is very crucial on your journey to the fulfillment of your purpose. Never do the following:

a. Don't send them email blasts or junk emails. If you must send them emails, personalize them.

b. Don't do mass email forwarding.

c. Don't do text blast to them.

d. Don't drop their names with anyone except when it is absolutely necessary. The moment they know that you drop their name in frivolous matters, they could withdraw from you. An example of this could be, "I was having breakfast with so and so yesterday," just to feel important.

e. Don't bombard them with calls, texts or emails (you may be perceived as a pest). For instance, I cannot imagine myself doing one or all of the points above to someone like Brother Kenneth Copeland or my spiritual father, Pastor E. A. Adeboye. You should not even do those to your friends except they don't mind, let alone a privileged relationship.

A privileged relationship in this context is a relationship with someone you respect because of the level of God's grace on his or her life and the volume of their work. The truth is, successful people are always very busy. Success is relative, depending on your definition. The point is, you too are successful and you must learn to respect yourself. You don't want people to start avoiding you or see you as a person who is not serious. Serious minded people will not be sending junk emails or irrelevant text messages to everybody on their contacts every day.

If people see you as somebody who has not added any perceived value to them because you have wasted their time in the past, the day you do have something valuable, they may see it as one of those jokes. I guess the point is clear: Communicate directly with busy people only when it is necessary, that way, they will also respect you. Some of the times you may consider communicating with them after asking for the best form of communication they prefer (e-mail, text, phone call etc.) include the following.

a. Wedding anniversary

b. Birthdays

c. When you want to give them gifts

d. When you have something valuable to offer them that could take their vision to another level.

When you are perceived as a person of value, they will give you more space into their private life where you will begin to discover more of the secrets responsible for their greatness. Don't forget, we all need strategic people to fulfill our purpose.

Even with these set of people, who may be ignorantly abusing the relationship, it is our responsibility to go extra miles to do our best within the grace of God to win them over to the right path. Cutting off or deliberately refusing to relate with them should usually be the last resort. Even when we do not relate with them again, it should not come to a point that we deliberately avoid them or wish them evil.

I know most people reading this book will probably say the usual cliché "I don't have anything against him. I just don't want to have anything to do with him again..." It is the easiest and most pious thing to say. However, I have discovered from my own personal life and others that it is actually possible to forgive somebody and not forget. Forgetting certain offenses is not possible depending on the gravity except someone has a memory loss. For example, it is almost impossible for a woman to forget her best friend who "snatched" her husband.

The true definition of forgive and forget is when the offended person has intentionally forgiven the offender to a point that the remembrance of that offence does not hurt anymore. This is the practical, realistic definition of forgive and forget. Of course, there are other minor offenses that could be wiped out completely from the memory as well. You probably can forgive and remove from your memory your roommate that stole one dollar from your wallet when you were in High School in 1970. This is different from telling a woman to completely wipe out the memory of her husband's adultery that produced a son who is now living with them especially when she has not had her own child.

In this case, the proof of her forgive and forget analysis will be that she now sees that child as her own and she is not hurt again. I could go on to give more explanations, but let us look at the following real life, check list of forgive and forget. I call them THE ACID TESTS OF GENUINE LOVE.

These questions are crafted to help you do an honest, objective appraisal of your love walk with people you have stopped relating with because of offense. As long as we remain on this terrestrial divide, we will all be offended. Not that offense may come, but that it WILL come.

The question is not IF but WHEN. They are guaranteed. In some cases, the higher you go and the deeper the relationship, the more painful and frequent the offenses. Jesus said, it is part of the characteristics of the last days (Matt. 2:4).

Acid Test #1: How do you feel when you hear of their progress? Happy, sad, or indifferent?

Acid Test #2: Sincerely speaking, what will be the state of your emotion if something terrible happens to them? Happy, sad, or indifferent?

Acid Test #3: If you see them by chance on the TV, will you change the channel regardless of what they may be talking about?

Acid Test #4: Imagine you meet at the aisle of a shopping mall suddenly, how will you feel? Will your heart race rapidly or skip a bit?

Acid Test #5: Would you send them a check to support their vision? Yes or No?

Acid Test #6: Will you accept a gift from them too? Yes or No?

If the answers to the questions above are suggesting that you will be indifferent or not exactly excited at their progress, there is a problem. Also, if the answers to the questions suggest that you are indifferent or happy at their calamity, there is a major problem. The following destructive negative emotions are already eating you up:

1. There is a chance that you have bitterness, anger, unforgiveness and resentment.

2. You may develop an internal crisis that is capable of causing stress related diseases like ulcer, hypertension, heart attack, and other deadly diseases.

3. You may no longer be in control of your own life. Whenever you get angry over everything that somebody does to you, that person is the one controlling your life. Your unforgiveness or bitterness has given them access into your life as your tormentors-in-chief (remember, they don't have to be around you or even know that they are tormenting you).

4. It may be an issue of arrogance or inadequate self image (ISI). People with this problem are usually very oversensitive. They also don't like people who disagree with them.

5. You may be wasting opportunities to contribute to their life what God has given you including the people they know and everyone in their circle of influence. It is like a chain. The point is, if the value you are bringing to the table is life-changing; imagine the number of people you are depriving. Also, remember the amount of money you are losing if they were to pay for what you have to offer.

6. The worst of it all is, you stand the risk of forfeiting the forgiveness of the only Person that matters in the final analysis, the Almighty God. Jesus said, *"If you don't forgive people, neither will my heavenly Father forgive you"* (Matt. 18:35). That sounds like hell. Now let's talk about the solutions.

PRACTICAL, DOABLE SOLUTIONS

1. Stop whatever you are doing and communicate with this person either through phone, emails, text, Facebook, Twitter etc. (He does not have to respond. At least you would have done your own part).
2. Pray for him sincerely.
3. You could send him a gift.
4. Stop saying negative things about him to other people.

In a perfect world, the above action steps should be enough to restore any genuine relationship but it doesn't always happen because most people are set in their ways. At this point, let it go. It will be their loss. You cannot in the name of peace and love, demean yourself. That will be against God's plan because nobody is supposed to play God in your life.

After you have genuinely practiced these four doable, practical solutions, you will begin to experience the following:

a. A sense of satisfaction
b. A sense of inner peace and tranquility

c. A sense of joy and excitement

d. A sense of prosperity and abundance

e. A sense of freedom and liberty

f. A sense of maturity

g. A sense of heaven on earth

h. A sense of God's approval

The relevance of this chapter to the fulfillment of your God ordained purpose is: You cannot truly fulfill purpose in isolation. Everybody has been sent to help other human beings. We are all interrelated. We will forever need one another except anybody who wants to be a hermit. The assumption that it is only God we need is a subtle excuse to endorse an arrogant, irresponsible, selfish lifestyle. It is not only fallacious, but hypocritical. Yes, we only need God when it comes to complete dependability. However, the Scripture says how can you claim to love God who you cannot see, and hate your brother? (1 John 4:20 paraphrased). I believe with all my heart that our gifts and purpose in life will explode to a whole new level when we start walking in a deeper level of God's love based on His word. That is my own personal desire and goal in life. I hope that's yours too.

To build a creative, successful platform for your gift and product in life, you need to consistently walk in love by faith.

BUILDING A PLATFORM THROUGH THE LAW OF HONOR

The law of honor says whatsoever you honor will honor and respect you with abundant blessing. This means you will attract whatever or whoever you honor. If you want to be prosperous, make every effort not to criticize those who are prosperous. If you want healing, don't criticize those who operate in the gifts of healings because you will eventually attract what you respect and honor. This law is similar to the law of sowing and reaping.

"(27)Then a man of God came to Eli and said to him, "Thus says the LORD: 'Did I not clearly reveal Myself to the house of your father when they were in Egypt in Pharaoh's house? (28)Did I not choose him out of all the tribes of Israel to be My priest, to offer upon My altar, to burn incense, and to wear an ephod before Me? And did I not give to

the house of your father all the offerings of the children of Israel made by fire? (29)*Why do you kick at My sacrifice and My offering which I have commanded in My dwelling place, and honor your sons more than Me, to make yourselves fat with the best of all the offerings of Israel My people?'* (30)*Therefore the LORD God of Israel says: 'I said indeed that your house and the house of your father would walk before Me forever.' But now the LORD says: 'Far be it from Me; for those who honor Me I will honor, and those who despise Me shall be lightly esteemed"* (1 Sam. 2:27-30).

The Scriptures above show how God views syncretism. God changed His mind concerning Eli the prophet, whose priesthood was supposed to be forever. That was the original plan of God for him but because he committed a ministerial blunder in not honoring God, the priesthood was taken away from his lineage. Every promise of God is conditional. For instance, marriage is a blessing from God but it is a fallacy to assume that you will experience the best of it regardless of how you treat your spouse. Honor begets honor.

You have to carry out your responsibility and also honor your spouse in order to enjoy the good thing that God has prepared for you in that marriage. God said those who honor Him, will be honored, and those who do not honor Him, will be lightly esteemed.

There are so many people who are successful according to the world's definition of success, but do not have anyone to share their wealth with. They end up living a cold and lonely life. Of what benefit is wealth when you don't have anybody to share it with? The beauty of wealth is to be able to give and impact the lives of those around us.

I heard the story of a man who was so wealthy but very wicked. One day, he threw a party and the people in the community refused to attend. Then, he woke up and realized that wealth which cannot be shared with people is vanity. It is not honorable. The morale of this story is: Life becomes more beautiful when people that are blessed use their God-given resources to lift up those who don't have. That to God is real wealth.

Study Guide

---

1. Write down the names of five people closest to you.

   a.

   b.

   c.

   d.

   e.

2. Identify their relationship with you in this order:

   a. Professional/business _____

   b. Spiritual _____

   c. Social _____

   d. All of the above _____

3. What have you contributed/given to these relationships since they started?

   a. Emotional _____

   b. Financial _____

   c. Spiritual _____

   d. Others _____

4. Are these relationships mutually beneficial? Evaluate the benefits on the lines below.

   _____

   _____

   _____

   _____

5. Identify five toxic relationships that you would like to re-evaluate (toxic relationships are those who take from you and break your focus in life).

    a.

    b.

    c.

    d.

    e.

6. Write down the names of five old friends that have been a blessing to you in the past and contact them regardless of their mistakes. If you are bitter and live in unforgiveness, you may not go far in life.

    a.

    b.

    c.

    d.

    e.

Chapter 13

THE THEORY OF REVERSE NEGATIVES

Creating Energy for Your Core Gift and Purpose

I read a funny but very educating cartoon many years ago. The cartoonist shows the picture of a weeping, helpless devil. A man walks by and asks, "Why are you shedding tears, Satan?" His response is, "These human beings are always accusing me of being responsible for every evil thing they go through, including their problems that are self inflicted."

No doubt, Satan is behind every evil thing but he cannot operate unless somebody allows him. I think too much credit is being given to the devil as if he is the one in charge of this world. Everything Jesus did is meant to strip the devil and his cohorts of their hold on us. It has remained our responsibility to enforce Jesus' victory and the devil's defeat. What the enemy uses today is fear, intimidation and perversion. That is why this chapter focuses on the theory of REVERSE NEGATIVES.

This is a theory God showed me while meditating in the word. It is based on the concept that because the devil cannot create anything, he can only reverse whatever God has created. The body of this theory is grounded and rooted in the Scriptures. God's nature of good is demonstrated throughout the Scriptures just like the devil's evil nature. Therefore, instead of concentrating on evil and struggling for the way out, and giving credit to Satan, the theory of REVERSE NEGATIVES teaches a system where the individual searches for the positive equivalent of the devil's perversion in the Bible by reversing it to what it was meant to be originally.

Most of the things you may consider as weaknesses are actually devil-organized perversions of God-given strengths when they are reversed in the light of God's word.

> *Most of the things you may consider as weaknesses are actually devil-organized perversions of God-given strengths when they are reversed in the light of God's word.*
> *Also, certain Godly, life-transforming emotions and habits that have been bastardized can be balanced using God's word.*

Also, certain Godly, life-transforming emotions and habits that have been bastardized can be balanced using God's word. Most of the times, perversion could be an overstretch of certain virtues where the individual loses control of where to apply the brake of balance. Almost everything that is good can become bad when over used, which inevitably could result into abuse. For example, food is good for the body but excessive eating could lead to overweight causing sickness in the process. Let's examine a few areas of weaknesses that could be reversed by applying the theory of REVERSE NEGATIVES.

1. Laziness is considered bad. Nobody wants to be referred to as lazy. Applying the law, laziness could be a perversion of rest. When people take vacation, it's supposed to be a time to unwind and rest. It only becomes laziness when it is not balanced with a good work ethic. Extreme rest will eventually lead to laziness.

2. Lousiness could be a perversion of exuberant joy. Have you seen individuals that are always very happy with life? They are expressive and energetic. It only becomes lousiness when it is not balanced with the relevant moods in each atmosphere per time. For instance, you will be considered lousy if you are laughing aloud with your whole body shaking vehemently inside a public library where others are reading. Therefore, exuberant, energetic joy, that is not balanced, could lead to lousiness.

3. Lust could be a perversion of genuine love. Most of the times, studies show that people caught up in illicit sex such as fornication, adultery are naturally nice people. Their inability to maintain proper balance is what is usually responsible for their down fall. The individual with this challenge is encouraged to reverse lust back to genuine, Godly love. That was God's original plan in his/her heart. A passionate love that is overstretched will eventually become lust.

4. Being rude or flippant may be a perversion of frankness or honesty. Individuals who tend to say things the way they are, because of their

temperamental make ups, are usually misunderstood as being rude. Maintaining a balance is recommended through the law of reverse negatives. It is not a good thing to be seen as being rude. It can impact your purpose negatively.

5. When a person talks a lot, he may be seen as garrulous. It might just be a God-given grace or skill. He could turn it to a profitable endeavor. He could become a lawyer, journalist or a professional trainer or speaker. The negatives associated with being perceived as a talkative can be reversed by deliberately and intentionally saying only things that are edifying.

6. Extravagance could be a perversion of generosity. If you give a lot to a point that it is becoming a wasteful spending, that may be a Godly generous spirit that is being perverted. Generosity should not get to a point when you squander all your life away. A lot of people, in an attempt to be there for everybody have almost unconsciously become everybody's bank only to wake up to the reality of life at old age. God wants us to be generous givers but not wasteful spenders. Our giving must be consistent, systematic and God inspired.

7. The opposite of generosity is also true. Certain people that are seen as stingy may be displaying the perverted version which is frugality. Being frugal and systematic in your giving is not only scriptural but will eventually make you wealthy. It allows you to save for investment opportunities while also giving generously to the funding of God's Kingdom. The extreme of careful giving is stinginess. The individual needs to apply this law of reverse negatives to maintain balance.

8. Being prideful may also be an overstretch of confidence. You need the virtue of confidence in the fulfillment of your life's purpose. However, arrogance may be the perversion of God-given confidence unless the law of reverse negatives is applied to curtail the extreme.

9. Depression could be a perversion of meditation on God's word or His goodness. People that are given to depression have mastered the art of analytical thinking.

> *Being prideful may also be an overstretch of confidence. You need the virtue of confidence in the fulfillment of your life's purpose. However, arrogance may be the perversion of God-given confidence unless the law of reverse negatives is applied to curtail the extreme.*

The only problem is, they meditate on negative experiences of their situations. The point is, it takes virtually the same time, energy and intellect to do negative and positive thinking. When the theory of reverse negatives is applied, the person flips the negative situation around by meditating on God's word and the sad experiences of life and depression become joy.

10. Passivity. Have you seen people that are so laid back that you almost think they do not want to engage in anything that looks difficult? In the past, I had castigated people for being so passive. With the law of reverse negatives, being laid back or being passive could just be a perversion of peace which is a virtue that is desirable. However, sometimes, to attain a lasting peace, you have to fight. Passive people should be encouraged to fight for peace.

11. Control and manipulation may be a perversion of dominion. It is interesting to know that the desire to reign in life and exercise dominion is innate in everybody. God put it in everyone in Genesis 1:26-29. When the desire to be in control of life gets to the point where other human beings are being controlled or manipulated, it becomes an abuse. When the law is applied, human control is reversed and real dominion (fulfilling your life's purpose) becomes automatic.

12. Fear. A negative weapon in the hands of the devil could be a perversion of an attempt to be careful sometimes. The other associates of fear such as worries, anxieties are all designed to move us away from a good virtue of careful planning, meticulous, reasonable thinking. For instance, it is not out of place to plan for retirement and other eventualities for the future, but when it becomes a concern that is getting to the borderline of worries and anxieties, then fear sets in. When the theory of reverse negatives is applied, the perversion is reversed to the positive which is careful planning based on God's word.

13. Humanism. The new age teaching that fundamentally addresses the power of the human mind and what it can achieve is an extreme desire to understand the capacity of the infinite wisdom of God. While it is a fact that the human mind is extremely complex in terms of its ability, it is still infinitely inferior to the mind of Christ that every believer possesses. (1 Cor. 2:16). Therefore, any attempt to want to tap into the human mind without God will be a perversion of the mind of Christ. I believe an averagely intelligent born-again person can reverse this

perversion by believing God to activate the mind of Christ that he has.

14. Idolatry. Every idol worship, whether they are inanimate objects or human beings, is a perverted attempt to search for the only, true God. Paul encountered certain idol worshippers in Athens who had an inscription on their idol "to the unknown god" (Acts 17:23). He took advantage of the same sentence, reversed it around and showed them the living God.

In every human being is a desire to worship, to fill the void. Unfortunately, because people have not been told what to do, they try to fill this void in their soul with drugs, sex, money, fame, success and even charities. The honest truth though is, only the true living God, who put that desire there can fill the void through Jesus Christ His Son and the Savior (John 14:6). The importance of the theory of Reverse Negatives is predicated on this simple premise.

1. If you beat yourself to death through negative criticisms to a point that you don't see anything good in yourself, life can be miserable until you apply this law.

2. You will soon discover that you are not as bad as you think. This is not an attempt to lower the standards but to expose the devil who is the accuser of the brethren.

3. There will be a new release of energy and grace for the fulfillment of your purpose. People become weak, confused and stranded when they think everything about them is evil. This is anti purpose. You need all the energy to engage your gifts for the achievement of your purpose.

4. The more you focus on the virtues (fruits of the spirit) the better you become. You become better with whatever you practice every time (James 1:25).

5. You don't wait until you become perfect before you start engaging your gift for your purpose. God perfects you in the process (2 Cor. 7:1).

6. The theory helps you put Satan where he belongs. He is not a creator, he is a master pervert. Since you know his strategy, always flip around whatever he suggests in the light of God's word. For instance, if he says you'll die, it means you will live. If he intimidates you with failure, success is very close. Don't give him any credit. He is a defeated foe.

Your understanding and application of this law is imperative in your journey to destiny. The table below gives a summary of how to practically apply the law.

The Theory of Reverse Negatives
Table 3

NEGATIVES	POSITIVES	PRACTICAL APPLICATIONS	BALANCE THROUGH SCRIPTURES
1. Laziness	Rest	Be diligent with your gifts everyday and rest	Proverbs 28:29
2. Lousiness	Exuberant Joy	Study the mood of the atmosphere and be moderate	Philippians 4:4-5
3. Lust	Passionate Love	Create reasonable boundaries	1 Thessalonians 4:3-6
4. Rudeness	Frankness/ Honesty	Learn to be firm and respectful	Romans 12:10
5. Garrulity (Talkativeness)	Communication Skill	Only speak words that build people up	Ephesians 4:29
6. Extravagance	Generosity	Be guided by God and His word in your giving	1 Corinthians 16:1-2
7. Stinginess	Frugality	Make all the money you can. Save all you can. Give all you can.	Deuteronomy 8:18 Philippians 4:19

8. Arrogance	Confidence	Respect other people's opinion, but never put yourself down.	Romans 12:10 Numbers 13:33
9. Depression	Capacity to Meditate in God's Word	Make sure what you think about always lines up with God's word	Philippians 4:8
10. Passivity (being laid back)	Desire for Peace	Fight for your heritage and relax.	Philippians 4:6-7
11. Control / Manipulation	Dominion	Gauge your life on this principle: Is it about me or other people.	Genesis 1:26-28
12. Fear	Being Careful	When it is fear, it is the devil. When it is planning, it is God.	2 Timothy 1:7
13. Humanism	Desire to operate in the mind of Christ	If Christ is not in the center of it, it is humanism. When Christ is involved, it is His mind.	Genesis 11:1-4 1 Corinthians 2:16
14. Idol Worship	A search for the True God	If it involves a lot of works, rituals and legalism, it is idolatry. When it involves the true Christ, there is peace.	Romans 7:14-25 Romans 8:1-6

Study Guide

---

1. Discuss the major components of the theory of Reverse Negatives with your study group.

2. For those who are too hard on themselves to a point that they cannot see anything positive, what are the three things you will recommend to them?
   a.
   b.
   c.

3. Identify five common negative emotions and how to reverse them.
   a.
   b.
   c.
   d.
   e.

4. Identify five of your strengths that could become weaknesses (negative) if you don't apply balance with Scriptures.
   a.
   b.
   c.
   d.
   e.

5. Discuss with your accountability group, the importance and relevance of the law of reverse negatives for the achievement of your purpose.

Chapter 14

LOOKING FOR THE LIVING IN THE MIDST OF THE DEAD

Creative Marketing System

It was 3:30 p.m. on that Thursday afternoon in the suburb area of the windy city of Chicago, IL. I had gone to a conference with two of our associate pastors and my executive assistant. The four of us were a little tired from the flight from Baltimore and were also hungry. I suggested we get something to eat on our way from the hotel to the venue of the conference. Upon inquiring from them which restaurant they preferred, Wilson, one of the Pastors responded "Old Country Buffet."

"How did you know there is one here?" I queried.

"Pastor, I saw their sign on our way from the airport," was his gentle response.

Through the help of the Global Positioning System (GPS) device in the rental car, we followed the signs advertising the restaurant. Four strangers from the East Coast paid good money for the delicious food Old Country Buffet offered us. It then suddenly occurred to me that strategic positioning and creative marketing system is imperative for sustainable growth of whatever you have to offer.

Your product or service is contending with similar products and services in the sea of thousands if not millions of products which is an interesting phenomenon. That is simply the reality of today's market place. It is an exciting time in the competitive global economy because the buyers and consumers are now having many options which create more innovations and creativity on the part of the producers. That to me is one of the benefits of capitalism.

The challenge is, no matter how valuable or indispensable your product is, if you don't advertise or market your brand, your voice will not be heard. It will be like whistling in the wind which does not necessarily translate to a defective or inferior product or service, it's just that people who need what you have to offer don't just know about you, your product or service. Even Jesus Christ our Lord and Savior emphatically inferred that you should not hide your light (whatever value you have) but you should place it where people can see it and be blessed by it, giving God the glory in the process.

> *The challenge is, no matter how valuable or indispensable your product is, if you don't advertise or market your brand, your voice will not be heard. It will be like whistling in the wind which does not necessarily translate to a defective or inferior product or service, it's just that people who need what you have to offer don't just know about you, your product or service.*

You should and must not limit your marketing strategies to word of mouth (WOM). Even though it remains one of the most viral effective tools there is, it has to be triggered by an experience predicated on a systematic marketing system and structure that is sustainable. This is very crucial because if the system can no longer sustain the viral explosion, that could be the end of the product. For instance, the Gadarene demon-possessed man who was delivered by Jesus through word of mouth campaign (testimony) brought Jesus' ministry to Decapolis (ten cities). Those thousands of people that were saved in those cities were effectively taken care of. Why should you advertise your brand or product if you do not have the infrastructure or system to supply the demand? You may need to consult experts in certain fields to help you as I did with this book.

I believe that Jesus' silent years before His public ministry were used by God to develop His character and to help Him design creative strategies to do His assignment.

It is my opinion that part of Jesus' marketing system was to train the first twelve men as His foot soldiers and then seventy whom He sent two by two into the marketplace of life before He would show up (some companies actually follow this method by testing the water before releasing their product to a particular market). That is not only smart but scriptural (remember the children of this world are wiser in their generation). The Queen of Sheba; a beautiful, magnificent, flamboyant, wealthy personality, heard of King Solomon's fame before coming to consult with him. How did she hear? Marketing. Joseph also marketed his brand to the butler "...don't forget me..." Why do you have companies spend billions on advertisement/marketing budgets during the Super bowl? Even CNN that is supposed to be a medium of advertisement is also marketing itself. It prides itself as "the most trusted name in the news." Nike's slogan is an adaptation of Jesus' mother's advice to the couple at the wedding reception; "Whatever He says to you, do it" (John 2:5). Going back to a sustainable, infrastructural system. This is about creating a resilient infrastructure that will accommodate the output of your marketing campaign.

Imagine a caterer who has been contracted to provide food and drink for 1,000 guests in a high profile society wedding reception of dignitaries from around the world. She has been referred to the couple by friends and her referral has been confirmed by a series of flyers and other marketing efforts. However, she, being so "spiritual," chooses to do a personal, twelve-hour all night prayer on Friday, the day preceding the wedding ceremony. She ends her prayer vigil at 8:00 a.m. and decides to take a nap. But because her body physiologically needs a deserved rest, she oversleeps and wakes up at 12 noon and the wedding reception starts at 2:00 p.m. At 1:00 p.m. the wedding planners start calling her cell phone and are being greeted each time with "this is Jessica, your favorite, one of a kind caterer, please leave a message..." (Jessica is a fictitious name, no reference to anyone in particular). Everyone is panicking but the couple however, is not in the loop yet to avoid distractions. At 2:30 p.m., it is obvious that something is not right. Then Jessica finally calls at 3:30 p.m. with lots of apologies stating that the food is on its way; also quickly adding a prayer that the devil's attack on that marriage will not hold (she is so spiritual, isn't it?). I am being sarcastic.

Meanwhile, the event coordinator has been secretly contacted to use frivolities to cover up by engaging the people in jokes, songs and emergency choreographies, to distract the guests from the reality at hand. But the guests, who could no longer be fooled, start dispersing.

Some having not eaten all day could not participate in a compulsory fast. A thousand guests turn to 980, then 400. In a short while, 400 become 250 and the food is still in transit. The wedding planners quickly arrange for a plan B from McDonald's, KFC, Subway and other fast foods. At 5:00 p.m., all the guests have left, except a few close friends and family members who are still hanging around to encourage the highly embarrassed couple. The new bride is wailing, yelling, cursing with smudged makeup due to tears coursing down like a rivulet on her rosy cheeks, thanks to Mary Kay. The groom is in anguish of soul but because "men should not cry" (whoever told them that lie), his internal crisis is only made visible by his red eyes and now tensed veins. Then the truck finally pulls into the parking lot at about 5:30 p.m. with food and drinks. You could smell the scintillating aroma from the truck, but it is too late, the guests are all gone. The food meant for a thousand people will now be served to only thirty people. The couple threatens to sue her for ruining their day. They can't however; because God might be "angry," after all, the caterer's ordeal is connected to the "all night prayer to God." Moreover, it must not be heard that a fellow sister is prosecuted on account of another brother or sister. That is the dilemma of our time.

This scenario informs us of one of the reasons why people, especially Christians do not prosper maximally in business. As long as you remain sloppy and warped in your strategies, you will always have handouts. In some cases the devil and his demons are not the culprits because Jesus dealt a great blow on them at Calvary. Failure in certain endeavors is a combination of several factors described in this book including laziness and lack of organizational skills.

Jessica, in our imaginative story, does not only lose this couple as clients for other ceremonies or functions but also loses a couple of hundreds of potential clients who would have engaged her service, had they had the chance to taste her delicious food. That could also have meant more referrals from them. The problem here is not the product, the ability, talents, or gifts but the inability to manage well. Gifts and talents are not enough. Unfortunately, as in most cases with good products and client satisfaction, negative spiral effects of a bad experience also travel fast through negative publicity.

As at the time of writing this book, Borders, the second largest bookstore chain in the U.S just filed for bankruptcy. Analysts say the reason why they crumbled is associated with lack of cutting edge, infrastructural online marketing system that is contextually relevant to the digital age. The book industry is no longer business as usual. Online book sales, according to experts, may now account for 70 percent of total sales in the U.S, leaving brick and mortal book stores to split the remaining 30 percent among themselves. Books-A-Million, Barnes & Noble, and other bookstore chains across the country are investing into their online categories every time. Authors, bookstores, and publishers who want to remain relevant must also add digital formatting and digital online promotion to their books. In fact, New York Times is in the process of launching the New York Times best seller versions of e-books. That is the future. You don't have to be a technical expert to get involved in the digital age (I'm not) but consult with those who understand this terrain; if you don't, you will be left behind. Don't be left in the past. Learn to live in the future from the present.

Anyone who finds himself/herself in a similar scenario like Jessica can only believe God by faith to reverse the situation because God is not just the God of second chance but many chances. Your Pastor may have declared over your life that you will be rich, but it is your responsibility to believe God for strategies to implement as you serve your gifts to the world. There is always a process between the prophetic declaration and its actual fulfillment. No prophecy will ever come to pass on its own. You need to play certain roles because God is not raising Zombies. You must be prepared. Les Brown, a professional speaker and best-selling author said, "It is not a tragedy to be prepared and not have an opportunity, but it is a tragedy not to prepare when the opportunity shows up." Think about that. If King David were alive today, Les Brown's statement would probably be his expertise. He really prepared before the opportunity showed up.

AMAZING STATISTICS ON CREATIVE MARKETING

Keller Fay Group, a research company, in a recent study discovered that 92 percent of people make their product decisions based on word of mouth otherwise known as WOM.

Also, for the first time in the history of the planet, the playing field is being leveled between the rich and the poor. Everybody now has equal access to the global village through the internet. Maggie Fox, partner, THE SOCIAL MEDIA GROUP said, "Social media has brought with it a complete disruption of traditional communication channels. What that means to the average person is that you no longer need to be a media baron or movie star or business mogul to get your name out there." Do you know that any creative, well packaged, relevant idea can generate multiple million hits in less than one month on YouTube? Think about that. The irrelevance of traditional means of communication is daily becoming obvious. As at the time of writing this book, 3,700 post office centers across the fifty States in the US are slated to close. The reason could be a digital disruption in the postal system. Who wants to wait for three to five days for snail mails to get their message across when we can send electronic mails (emails) in seconds? Snail-speed mails have become ineffective in a fast paced, revolutionary age.

What is marketing? The American Marketing Association (AMA) has just updated its definition, "Marketing is the activity conducted by organizations and individuals that operates through a set of institutions and processes for creating, communicating, delivering, and exchanging market offerings that have values for customers, clients, marketers, and society at large."

In the past, your success depended on who you knew, today that is changing. With creative, personal branding and a pro-active marketing system, it is who knows you.

Our world is evolving very rapidly. What was considered excellent a few years ago has become antiquated today. These dynamics are seen everywhere. In the past, your success depended on who you knew, today that is changing. With creative, personal branding and a pro-active marketing system, it is who knows you. Search engines are busy 24/7 with people searching for who could solve their problems whether tangible or intangible. It is also very scriptural. The twenty-first century man is trying to catch up with God's wisdom.

Most of the things we call new breakthroughs today happened long ago in Bible days.

Most of the people who benefited from the ministry of Jesus Christ heard about Him before they met Him. Whether it was the woman with the issue of blood or Zacchaeus who strategically positioned himself by climbing a tree, somehow they all heard about Jesus and His brand: The Savior and miracle worker.

This digital age is interesting for those who would take advantage of its positive platforms. Study these statistics.

- 84 percent of college students will be participating in social networks by the end of 2011 (Anderson Analytics, 2007)
- 50 percent of online adults will also be active in social networks (eMarketer, 2007)
- 18 percent of people will be active in social networks on mobile devices (eMarketer, 2007)

You can use podcast to showcase your talents, abilities, or gifts, such as a video presentation of your music, movies, dance, speaking engagements, etc. You cannot afford not to have a beautiful, functional website and get involved with at least one social network. Effective, pro-active marketing campaign will strategically position you, your brand and product. This is the point. Got it? I'm sure you do.

Study Guide

---

1. If you have only one core gift to market, what would it be? Write three reasons why you would choose this particular ability over others.

    a.

    b.

    c.

2. If you were given two minutes to explain your purpose in life and the gifts you would use to accomplish it, would you do it effectively?

3. Write down an elevator speech of your purpose in life.

4. The digital age and media have created a new kind of communication model. Discuss with your group.

5. a. There are so many marketing channels today, identify three of them that you think are most strategic to your gifts/products.

    i.

    ii.

    iii.

    b. What are your plans to maximize them?

6. What deliberate, intentional steps are you taking to get your brand and product out? Discuss three of these steps and evaluate their success relative to where you are going.

    a.

    b.

    c.

7. If your gift or product explodes as a result of your marketing effort, what structure do you have in place to ride the wave? Discuss. (Remember Jessica's story?)

Part Four

ON THE MOVE

Chapter 15

MARKETING IS SPIRITUAL

Overcoming Shame Associated with Marketing

The law of Publicity and Marketing states that whatever grace, gift, talent and ability that God has given to you must be publicly made available in the market place for the expansion of God's kingdom by adding value to humanity.

"(14)You are the light of the world. A city that is set on a hill cannot be hidden. (15)Nor do they light a lamp and put it under a basket, but on a lamp stand, and it gives light to all who are in the house" (Matthew 5:14-15).

According to this law, when you light a lamp, you must put it where it can benefit mankind. The law further states that whatever product or services you want people to benefit from must be accessible to them. The onus is on you to make your gifts and talents visible to the world. Don't put your inventions and creativity under the table; you must get it out to the people so that it can add value to them. That is what all the people in Hollywood and the entertainment industry are doing.

MARKETING IS AS OLD AS ANCIENT TIMES

The law of marketing, because of its universal nature, will work for anybody, regardless of their race, gender, religion or background.

"(1)Nebuchadnezzar the king made an image of gold, whose height was sixty cubits and its width six cubits. He set it up in the plain of Dura, in the province of Babylon (2)And King Nebuchadnezzar sent word to gather together the satraps, the administrators, the governors, the counselors, the treasurers, the judges, the magistrates, and all the

officials of the provinces, to come to the dedication of the image which King Nebuchadnezzar had set up [3]*So the satraps, the administrators, the governors, the counselors, the treasurers, the judges, the magistrates, and all the officials of the provinces gathered together for the dedication of the image that King Nebuchadnezzar had set up; and they stood before the image that Nebuchadnezzar had set up* [4]*Then a herald cried aloud: "To you it is commanded, O peoples, nations, and languages,* [5]*that at the time you hear the sound of the horn, flute, harp, lyre, and psaltery, in symphony with all kinds of music, you shall fall down and worship the gold image that King Nebuchadnezzar has set up"* (Daniel 3:1-5).

This heathen king's goal was to make sure that the whole world bowed down to his golden image. He applied this law of marketing and publicity by getting the services of a herald (marketing or publicity consultant) to announce his product (golden image). He got people to blow trumpets and play all kinds of music. Everybody came from all over to bow to the graven image. At that time, Babylon was the equivalent of what America is today, and so anything that was in Babylon was considered very good. Although the king's intent was anti- God, people still came from all over the world to bow to the image; this is because the law of publicity and marketing will work for anybody. It is a universal law.

The Bible says, *"Let your light so shine before men, that they may see your good works and glorify your Father in heaven"* (Matthew 5:16). Even though in this Scripture, Jesus was primarily talking about character and godliness, the word of God has multidimensional meanings. The Scripture is also talking about feeding the poor, clothing the naked and all the other good things you can do to make the world a better place. The Bible is full of metaphors describing certain words.

In fact, some particular words in the Scriptures have been defined by four or five metaphors. For example, the word of God can be described as a hammer, a seed, a sword and as the bread of life, to mention a few. Does that mean you see a lamp or a sword in God's word? No. It is just a symbol; a metaphor to describe what the word of God is and what it can do. Looking at the literal meaning of God's word can be myopic because beyond the surface, the word of God has more to say. The "light" Jesus is talking about here could be your creativity, products, ideas or whatever you have to bring to the consumers. In the context of this book, light represents the abilities, skills, and services that God has given to you to bless humanity. Maybe your gift is preaching, public speaking, running a business or writing. You need to learn how to package and brand your ideas. You must also understand how to create a market for your core gift and make it available.

Light in the words of Jesus is a harbinger of hope. It symbolizes knowledge, revelation and civilization. Light is a product, a valuable gift, an ability or witty invention that is given to you by God to bless your world. How will people know that you are a great singer if they do not have access to your DVDs and CDs?

> *Light in the words of Jesus is a harbinger of hope. It symbolizes knowledge, revelation and civilization. Light is a product, a valuable gift, an ability or witty invention that is given to you by God to bless your world. How will people know that you are a great singer if they do not have access to your DVDs and CDs?*

The potential consumers of your gifts are in the marketplace and are searching for something authentic and tangible. Your prayer and fasting must therefore be converted into something that people can see and touch. Jesus said don't hide your light under the table. How can you hide your ideas when you can publish it to the whole world, bless them and fulfill your purpose in the process?

Jesus said "*let your light so shine…*" He didn't say "let God shine your light." Jesus said I have made you the light of this world but it is your responsibility to shine your light. Jesus wants you to do something about it so your creativity can shine before men. The question to always ask is: would that witty invention, business idea, or product bless humanity and glorify God?

"*(14)You are the light of the world. A city that is set on a hill cannot be hidden. (15)Nor do they light a lamp and put it under a basket, but on a lamp stand, and it gives light to all who are in the house*" (Matt. 5:14-15).

In the modern day twenty-first century language, what the Scripture is saying is this, you need to shine your light through every means available. The law of publicity otherwise referred to as advertising or marketing can also be called the law of strategic positioning.

"[1]Then Jesus entered and passed through Jericho [2]Now behold, there was a man named Zacchaeus who was a chief tax collector, and he was rich [3]And he sought to see who Jesus was, but could not because of the crowd, for he was of short stature [4]So he ran ahead and climbed up into a sycamore tree to see Him, for He was going to pass that way [5] And when Jesus came to the place, He looked up and saw him, and said to him, "Zacchaeus, make haste and come down, for today I must stay at your house" (Luke 19:1-5).

Zacchaeus was so desperate to see Jesus, but because he was a short man, he had to position himself in such a way that Jesus could see him. In today's language that would be marketing. What does marketing do? It allows people to see you and what you have to offer.

Zacchaeus ran and climbed the sycamore tree; he must have done his due diligence, so he knew that Jesus was going to come in that direction. He was not a lazy man. He did his research very well. How did Jesus see him? He saw him because he strategically positioned himself.

It is very naïve of us to think that just because God gave us an idea, the whole world would automatically know about it. Isn't it weird for a person to be in business without a business card or some sort of advertisement? How would you sell your product if people don't know about it? Coca-Cola is the most popular brand name on the planet as a result of cutting edge, aggressive marketing.

In fact, I heard a very disturbing statistics some years ago and I made up my mind that I was going to use everything God has given me to go to the ends of the earth in search of souls. The statistics indicated that Coca-Cola was more popular than the name of our Lord Jesus Christ. Coca-Cola is in every city and village on earth. Think about the power of marketing.

Some missionaries went to evangelize in an African country many years ago, and asked the people in a particular neighborhood if they knew about Jesus. Sadly enough, they innocently replied that they didn't know about anybody with that name and didn't even know when He moved into their neighborhood! They were hearing about that name for the first time. The dynamics of our world have become more complex. The world is becoming more visual. No matter how brilliant or valuable your products and services are, you will still need to market because people always respond to what they see. In January 2010, after the earthquake in Haiti, the media blew up everything. Information that would take months in the past for people to find is now taking a few seconds and minutes because of the power of the internet and cutting edge media outlets. As a result, millions of people and organizations donated their money and resources to help Haiti. People were watching the devastation live. The news spread in a jiffy, because there was a twenty-four hour media coverage of the aftermath of the disaster. What do you think would have happened if there was no means of getting the information across? Several hundreds of people would have been trapped in the rubble. People all over the world are becoming more publicity driven. This is one of the main reasons you should give a face to your ideas, abilities, and talents. Joseph marketed his gifts and dreams.

He added value to the baker by interpreting his dreams. But he said something that many believers today will not say. *"When Pharaoh restores you, please remember me."* What do you think he was doing? He was marketing himself. He was asking for a referral. He was not just praying and wishing and hoping. What is a referral? A referral is simply when you ask a person to tell somebody about you, your services or products. The butler actually forgot him for two years, but the same man remembered him afterwards. What if Joseph had not asked the man for a referral? Also, Esther, a paragon of beauty, was an icon when it comes to excellence.

This woman was so captivating and charismatic. She was not just a naturally beautiful person, her passion was to invade the kingdom of this world with the mentality of heaven and she knew that God had positioned her in that palace for a purpose. There was a time when she wanted to see the king on behalf of her people after fasting and praying. Guess what she did? She dressed in her royal apparel; I believe she probably used perfume and deodorant before going in to meet the king. She marketed herself well and she did not fool herself by saying because she prayed and fasted, everything was going to be alright. She did what was naturally required of her, after she settled the matter spiritually.

Esther preserved her people with the anointing of the Holy Spirit and her marketing strategy. She knew the purpose of her beauty and she used it to the advantage of God's kingdom to save a whole generation. The king lost his balance on seeing her. Why? The Bible says *"(1)The king's heart is in the hand of the LORD, like the rivers of water; He turns it wherever He wishes"* (Prov. 21:1), but you must be ready to present your gifts, so that the king can see it. The King in this context could also be a strategic person that will support what you are offering.

You need to maximize everything which God has endowed you with, by using every available modern technology. Make the most of the internet, radio, television, flyer, referrals, cards, Facebook, Twitter, and word of mouth. Use everything to get your products out. Add life to the valuable things you are presenting to your world. Jesus, the Son of God understood the law of making His endowments available as mentioned in the Scriptures below.

"(18)The Spirit of the LORD is upon Me, because He has anointed Me to preach the gospel to the poor; He has sent Me to heal the brokenhearted, to proclaim liberty to the captives and recovery of sight to the blind, to set at liberty those who are oppressed; (19) To proclaim the acceptable year of the LORD" (Luke 4:18-19).

Jesus seems to be saying;

The spirit of God is upon me and I know what to do with it. Acts 10:38 confirms His proclamation. *"How God anointed Jesus of Nazareth with the Holy Spirit and with power, who went about doing good and healing all who were oppressed by the devil , for God was with Him."*

Jesus went about serving His products to bless humanity and God confirmed it with signs and wonders.

"And He said to them, "Go into all the world and preach the gospel to every creature" (Mark 16:15).

The greatest of all services or products is the gospel of the Kingdom. Jesus said, *"go into all the world and preach the gospel,"* but we want the world to come into the church; our store to purchase or to get the product that we are offering. But the owner of the product wants us to go and give it to His "clients" outside the church.

What is the product of the church? It is Kingdom of God through Jesus Christ. There is nothing like the message of Jesus. That is the gospel that will save the worst sinner; because His blood will cleanse the dirtiest sin.

Think of what would have happened if apostle Paul had the kind of modern day media outlets. He would have bombarded all of them with the gospel of God's grace. Let us preach this gospel with passion. Let us go into the entire world and save souls. If you really think you have something valuable to offer the world, why would you keep it to yourself ? That is unfair.

It's like somebody who just discovered plenty of food and water in an oasis in a desert and refuses to tell his fellow travelers until they die of starvation and thirst. Be like the lepers who discovered a huge bounty of foods and resources in their twilight and came back to their fellow country men and women to advertise their discovery.

My friend, you have something to brand and market, it could be your story of how you conquered a particular terminal disease or the story of a family triumph over divorce, or how you have successfully lived with the same spouse for fifty years. Such stories are needed in today's world where the average life span of marriage now is two years.

Bottom line is; there are millions if not millions of people all over the world who need your contribution to their lives, but they are being deprived of your solution because they do not know your solution exists. Shameful, isn't it. This is not an attempt to blackmail you emotionally, but it is my straight forward way of telling you how desperate we are willing to partake of God's grace on your life.

> *Bottom line is; there are millions if not billions of people all over the world who need your contribution to their lives, but they are being deprived of your solution because they do not know your solution exists. Shameful, isn't it.*

Therefore, write that book, release those songs, bring out those inventions, transfer that anointing and grace to the new generation. When you do, let the whole world know about it. Don't be like Elisha who went into the grave with God's grace. The grave is already a rich place, don't add to that unneeded deposit of wealth; we need you now or never.

Study Guide

---

1. Write down in the space below the Law of Marketing.

2. The Law of Marketing and Publicity is universal and will work for anybody regardless of their race, culture or color. Discuss this statement with three examples.

   a.

   b.

   c.

3. "Light" in God's word could be your idea, gift, resources, talents or creativity. Discuss with your study group.

4. Marketing is also described as strategic positioning. Zacchaeus demonstrated this assertion in Luke 19. Discuss the relevance of this story with your study group.

5. One element of marketing is referral. Discuss how Joseph effectively used this in the prison.

6. The demon-possessed man that was set free in Mark 5 advertised the ministry of Jesus in ten cities. Discuss with your group the viral nature of word of mouth in marketing.

Chapter 16

LEVERAGING YOUR EXPERTISE, PLATFORM, AND SUCCESS

Giants Living In The Shadow

I CAN DO ALL THINGS

There is more to life than where you are now. There is always a better lifestyle, a healthier life, a better marriage; a better way of doing what you may be thinking is your full maximum potential. You've got to be intentional and deliberate in leveraging your expertise, platform and success.

A lot of people don't know that success or achievement in life in a particular endeavor can be used to achieve the same or even a greater level of success in other areas of life as well. This is what leveraging is all about.

To leverage means to exert power or influence. It is the power or ability to influence people. It is taking a positive advantage garnered over the years through hard work, integrity, and life changing contributions you have made into people's life.

> *To leverage means to exert power or influence. It is the power or ability to influence people. It is taking a positive advantage garnered over the years through hard work, integrity, and life-changing contributions you have made into people's life.*

A systematic leveraging will most of the time have the following components.

1. Your Platform: A body of principles in which you take a stand for your conviction and the medium/media being used to carry it out.

2. Your Experience: Knowledge or practical wisdom gained from what you have personally observed in life.

3. Integrity: Your character and value system.

4. Brand: What makes you stand out from the crowd? Your uniqueness.

5. Your Expertise: Your skills set.

6. Your Love Walk: The positive, value adding relationship you have with people.

7. Your Success: The positive outcome or results of your endeavors.

All these components would allow for a smooth leveraging of your gifts or products into other areas. As it has been noted in the previous chapters, studies show that an average person has more than two or three main gifts. God wants you to maximize your core unique gift, but He also wants you to take advantage of the other gifts too. In fact, one of the central key points of this book is to show you how to first of all focus aggressively on your core gift until you become a voice with expertise, platform, and success, then leverage your achievements into the other areas where you are equally gifted or passionate. This to me is real purpose.

In my experience in dealing with highly successful people and those who may be considered less successful, I have come up with three conclusions.

1. Some of the highly successful people don't know that they can be more successful by using their success to achieve more success in other areas.

2. Some who are successful and are taking advantage of leveraging for more success but who cannot impact or teach the principles in a systematic way for others to use. In other words, they understand what they do but do not have a system like books, CDs, DVDs, or programs that other people can follow. So their success becomes a mystery. Some of them even mystify their achievements when they are asked "what is the secret of your success" by responding,

"the grace of God." My understanding of the grace of God is that it is available to all. Systematic leveraging makes progress predictable.

3. My third conclusion has to do with those who have several abilities and gifts, and who are trying to leverage them into different areas at the same time and their lives start falling apart because they are coming under pressure. This chapter focuses on the pro-active dynamics of leveraging.

To leverage also means to exert a certain amount of energy or resources to accomplish multiple tasks at different times so that you conserve your energy or resources for other parts of the business. The goal is to save energy or resources so you can focus on what is more important to you.

> *When you are just starting out at the beginning of any enterprise, you will have more time than money to invest, so invest it aggressively. Soon you'll begin to experience the reverse, where you will have more money than time, that's when you start thinking of leveraging both your time and money. That is when you become issues rich and time broke.*

When you are just starting out at the beginning of any enterprise, you will have more time than money to invest, so invest it aggressively. Soon you'll begin to experience the reverse, where you will have more money than time, that's when you start thinking of leveraging both your time and money. That is when you become issues rich and time broke. You'll have to start hiring other people to complete your tasks for you so that you can invest your time, money, and energy in other places. The beautiful thing is that, the other areas of endeavor you may be considering for leveraging are usually the expertise or core intelligence of other people. For example, if I decide to start a television network in the future after I have successfully maximized my core gift, I will likely attract professionals in the media whose core intelligence is broadcasting. So my leverage becomes their expertise. Talk about a win-win situation. This concept runs through life even to the minutest details. We all need one another.

Why is it important for you to build a platform, success and develop your expertise and brand before you start thinking about other endeavors? The answer is simple. People want to do business with perceived authority, specialists or experts.

Our world today is expert or specialist driven. For instance, if you have a terrible legal case, would you want somebody just coming out of law school to handle it or somebody with a certain level of expertise? Also, no one suffering from a potentially dangerous disease will go to a medical student but will prefer to go to a specialist. This principle applies to every industry.

Therefore, if you are a professional in any endeavor and you are experiencing certain relative success, you could extend your influence and expertise through writing, speaking, or consulting. Your expertise, platform and success will give you an advantage in a new endeavor.

Even if you are not a professional, your particular story could motivate or inspire people to come out of the woods. The uniqueness of your story as a housewife, student, pastor, or businessman may be what some people need to move to the next phase of their endeavors.

This is the sequence of a systematic, creative leveraging.

Identify your core gift or intelligence ——> Develop it through constant target practice and branding ——> become an expert at it ——> create a platform or following ——> become successful.

Significance or meaning occurs at the point when you extend your expertise, platform and success into other endeavors for the purpose of spreading your influence to help others. This is called systematic, creative leveraging.

In addition to the expertise of various professionals that you may want to engage, you also want to check out their track records (experience, history), integrity (character), their platform and maybe their testimonies.

Leveraging, like other concepts being used in the contemporary world, is not new to God. He started it all. David is a classical example of a man who really took advantage of his expertise, track record, and success. He referred to the testimony of how he killed a bear and a lion in the wilderness and that he was going to kill Goliath in the same manner. It was not a coincidence that he used the same fighting strategies and equipment to kill Goliath.

"Your servant has killed both lion and bear; and this uncircumcised Philistine will be like one of them, seeing he has defied the armies of the living God" (1 Sam. 17:36).

His military strategy in fighting war by depending on God would later be leveraged into government. In the hearts of the people, it was like "if this man could risk his life for animals and risk his life to kill Goliath, he alone deserves to be our leader...."

I also want to believe that his expertise, platform, and success contributed immensely to the inspiration he had when he was writing those songs in the book of Psalm. When successful people sing, people will listen.

A time will come when you will have been so successful with your current core gift deployment that God will create new platforms for you to leverage. However, it would be your responsibility to follow His instructions to venture into other passions you have with the objective of being a blessing. To avoid the danger of over stretching yourself in an attempt to leverage, you have to trust God for the wisdom to do it effectively and efficiently. Some of the things you might consider include the following.

1. Creating a system that is dependable, repeatable, and turnkey. Somebody aptly gave the acronym for "system" as Saves You Stress, Time, Energy and Money.

2. Automation. Take advantage of the digital age and the technologies it has to offer. Use contact manager to maintain contact with people in your online community. Use auto responder. Put the system to work on an auto pilot mode.

3. Make your expertise teachable after creating a signature system or product that makes you stand out. For example, if you order a book tonight on Amazon, Jeff Bezos, the CEO, is not the one you are dealing with. You are interacting with a turnkey system that is efficient.

4. Simplify complex ideas, concepts and your approach, and they will help you simplify your life.

WAYS TO LEVERAGE YOUR EXPERTISE, PLATFORM, AND SUCCESS

1. **Publication:** Everybody has a story to tell. It could be the story of how you supernaturally conquered a terminal disease contrary to doctors' claims that you will die within a few weeks, or how you became prosperous in what you are doing now. You do have certain experiences in life that can benefit other people. I once humorously encouraged my wife to write a book on *How To Live With A Difficult Man While Still Loving Him*.

2. **Electronic:**
   a. You could put your story, products or service on DVDs.
   b. You could put them in movies.
   c. You could do coaching and consulting.
   d. You could do the same with CDs and DVDs.
   e. You could put them on your website.
   f. You could put them on MP3 players.

3. **Live Presentation:** You could organize live conferences and seminars. Bottom line, the world is waiting for what you got!

4. **Franchise:** The franchise mode of business represents hundreds of industries that you can take advantage of. Go to franchisedirect.com.

5. **New Business:** You could start a new business altogether on your brand name and hire people to run it.

6. **Endorsement:** This is putting your brand name on a particular product. The advantage of this is that you only do it one time. This is very popular with famous athletes and celebrities.

7. **Venture Capitalism:** This is providing funds to early stage, high potential growth, startup companies. The venture capitalist makes money by having equity ownership of such companies. Usually, certain percentages after a third party, unbiased, valuation has been done. Most wealthy people of the world are venture capitalists. They have learned how to make money work for them. Because of its risky nature, professional advice is usually sought from experts before embarking on such ventures.

8. **Complete Exit From Your Core:** You can also venture into a new arena of endeavor entirely by taking a complete exit from your core gift after retirement. This is advisable for sports people and athletes. You cannot be active forever. You can sustain injury or may not be agile anymore because of old age.

9. **Human Capital:** Another area you can leverage is your relationship equity. This is an arena that can be ignored easily because it is not tangible. Yet it is a great blessing if you are a lovable person. Some people in your circle of influence can loan you money to start a business or introduce you to people that could show you a line of business. They could say one sentence that could change your life forever.

I have been privileged to enjoy this type of leverage. By God's grace, I have had occasions to introduce certain church members to my rich friends who showed them how certain businesses are done. As a result, their lives have changed forever.

It has been said that everybody is just about two to four people away from an influential person. For instance, I am just two people away from President Barack Obama, if meeting him is part of my destiny. How? Bishop Ken Fuller is my friend. Bishop Fuller is close to Dr. Creflo Dollar who knows President Obama. You can practice this; it will amaze you that you are not far from greatness. But more importantly, I personally know the Almighty God who also knows me. We talk everyday and fellowship every time. All the glory goes to Jesus who made it possible. To me, that is the best relationship equity.

BENEFITS OF STRATEGIC LEVERAGING

1. Multiplication of Influence: When you spread your worth into other spheres of life, you multiply your influence and value systems thereby giving more people an opportunity to connect to the grace of God upon your life.

2. You Give Advantage to Others: Many people will struggle in life endlessly without the help of other successful people. The number one reason why God would allow you to succeed in life is so that you could use your successful platform to lift up other struggling people.

For instance, giving a timely endorsement to a startup company or organization after evaluating their value system is a great way to leverage. Your name and integrity can make a difference in their turn over.

3. Multiple, Passive Residual Income: Leveraging into other endeavors also allows you to earn consistent, passive residual income. Real wealth is exhibited when you have multiple streams of income coming in regularly, whether you work or not. If you have to work every time to earn your money, you are trading hours for dollars which is good. The only problem with it is that you don't get paid except when you trade your time. So what happens to you if for instance, you could not work for three months? I believe it is reasonable for anyone to get involved in one or two ventures that can generate income regardless of whether they work or not. Some experts actually recommend at least five streams of income. You may need to refer to the different ways to leverage discussed earlier. Passive residual income is the money that comes in every now and then as a result of what you only did one time or what others are doing on your behalf. That is leveraging the efforts of other people. If David were alive today, he would probably be getting royalties from the songs he composed. We still read and sing them today.

4. Life of Peace and Significance: Perhaps the greatest advantage of leveraging is when you get to a point where money doesn't have to be the factor to consider when God is asking you to bless somebody or give to the Kingdom. Granted that regardless of your status in life financially, the faith walk is an everlasting commitment (you have to believe God for everything), but I also believe that you can creatively set up a Holy Spirit inspired system that God would use to funnel the funds to you on a consistent basis. Creating that system in my own opinion is also an act of faith. Even for preachers and ministers who have been called with a divine mandate, people and not ghosts are the instruments God uses to "support" the work. But the more effective and efficient the systems are, the more encouraged and motivated the givers become.

For instance, we support a couple of ministries regularly. These ministries make it more convenient by creating efficient systems such as letters of appreciation, return stamped envelopes for future offerings, inspiring messages and in some cases DVDs or CDs of encouraging messages that stir our faith for the next level. These may look simple, but they could make the difference between success and failure. We also have a similar system in our ministry.

The key point of this chapter is: identify, develop, and deploy your core gifts and talents first until such a time when you have a platform and you become a successful expert at what you do, then you begin to prayerfully consider other areas to spread your influence.

In certain cases, this could be the other way around where you have a situation when other gifts or abilities were first discovered before the main gifts. If that is the case with you, you could focus on those "minor" gifts or abilities until you have some level of relative success that could then pave the way for the main/core gift.

There could be other occasions where two main/core gifts may be used interchangeably, especially if they are closely intertwined. Joseph used the gifts of dream and interpretation of dreams together. David used his musical gift at a point to drive out demons from Saul. I believe he used the same gift to write and sing the majority of the book of Psalms.

There have been instances where successful pastors and evangelists were inspired to resign to start major television networks or organizations that are reaching more people around the world. Dr. Oral Roberts, one of the foremost evangelists that ever walked this earth was also the founder of a university named after him. It is high time you started searching through the help of the Holy Spirit. You can never tell what He may instruct you to focus on and where to leverage. The same Paul who said *"This one thing I do…"* (Philippians 3:13) (Referring to his core gift), also said, *"I can do all things through Christ who strengthens me,"* (Philippians 4:13) (referring to his multiple intelligences).

The following are a few examples of notable people who leveraged their core intelligence into other areas of endeavors. It also includes people who systematically transitioned into their core intelligence by engaging the other gifts successfully.

1. Pastor Enoch Adeboye: From being one of the most successful pastors to a world class mentor and spiritual father to millions of people globally. He is one of the 100 most influential people in the world according to TIMES MAGAZINE.

2. Dr. John Maxwell: From being a successful pastor to a famous leadership expert.

3. Arnold Schwarzenegger: From a successful acting career in Hollywood to governor of California.

4. Nelson Mandela: From being a political activist to president of South Africa and now an elder statesman providing leadership.

5. Donald Trump: From real estate investment into media (The Apprentice).

6. Serena Williams: From tennis into fashion.

7. Dr. Myles Munroe: From pastoring to consulting for corporations and world leaders in government.

8. Dr. Oral Roberts: From a successful evangelistic ministry to education. Founder of Oral Roberts University. One of the most famous universities in the world.

9. Markus Lamb: From a traveling evangelist to being the founder of Daystar TV Network.

10. Dr. David Oyedepo: From being a successful pastor to being a chancellor of Covenant University, a renown private university.

11. Martin Luther King, Jr.: From a preacher to a historic civil rights leader.

12. What about you, from being _____ to _____.

Everybody should have a defining moment of their core gift when they say "this is one thing I do," and later transition by leveraging into other things, where they say "I can do all things."

I am grateful to God that I know where to focus on for this phase of my life—communicating the supernatural through speaking and writing and I know where to leverage later. Prominent among them are the media and the entertainment kingdoms. What about you?

Master that core intelligence of yours first and then systematically deploy it into other arenas so that you can boldly say like Paul that you have become all things to all men because it is at that state that you can prosper in all you do. There's nothing wrong in you being multi-talented because God really wants you to engage all your gifts. The same Paul who said *"this one thing I do…."* referring to his dominant gift also said, *"I can do all things through Christ"* referring to other gifts and abilities.

What you should avoid is to start stretching yourself too thin before you are rooted and well branded in your core gift. This can make you go around in circles for a long time, until your dominant gift becomes stale. That would be like somebody running on a treadmill—running on the same spot.

Study Guide

---

1. If you were to leverage your current success into other endeavors, what would they be? Identify four of those areas.

   a.

   b.

   c.

   d.

2. What would be the medium to use to leverage? Discuss four of them with your study group.

   a.

   b.

   c.

   d.

3. Write down four reasons for leveraging in your order of preference. Discuss them using the Bible and real life characters.

   a.

   b.

   c.

   d.

4. Discuss three definitions of leveraging and their relevance to your multi-giftedness.

   a.

   b.

   c.

5. Write down four reasons why you should focus on your main intelligence or core gift before thinking of leveraging.

   a.

   b.

   c.

   d.

6. An average human being has more than one ability or gift. Discuss.

7. Leveraging requires creative systems: Discuss them.

Chapter 17

WEALTH TRANSFER DEMYSTIFIED
Understanding God's Consistent Patterns

Events happening around the world such as economic recession, regional wars, civil unrests, earthquakes and other natural disasters are signs of the last days. But in the midst of these negative events are also positive signs that are part of eschatological discourse adumbrated in the Bible. For example, Jesus Christ said that there would be more marriages before the close of the age; that's positive, isn't it? While I do not claim to be an accurate eschatologist, the Bible is clear on the positive indications to look for. In addition to many marriages, Joel also prophetically declares;

"(28)And it shall come to pass afterward that I will pour out My Spirit on all flesh; your sons and your daughters shall prophesy, your old men shall dream dreams, your young men shall see visions. (29)And also on My menservants and on My maidservants I will pour out My Spirit in those days" (Joel 2:28-29).

That would be God's unusual grace to shake this earth before the Lord's return. The word "Apocalypse" is from a Greek word *Apokalypsis* which means "lifting the veil or revelation." It is "a disclosure of something hidden from the majority of mankind in an era dominated by falsehood and misconception." This chapter is therefore a peep into the prophetic destiny of the church through the help of the Holy Spirit and God's word.

What the world is going through now has always been the experience of anyone who declares independence with God. The devil, *"...the god of this age..."* (2 Cor. 4:4) (the systems of this world) is insidiously always on the rampage to wreck havoc. He has mastered his trade in such a way that even though he is not generous, he can give some freebies to his victims as long as he captures their souls forever. That explains one of the reasons why some rich people in this world are also some of the most preposterous in their ideology. Satan can also give apples, but in the end they will be full of worms. That is why nations that are in the vanguard of campaign of innuendos and Anti-Semitism are rich with oil and other natural resources. You may be wondering and asking, so what happens to God's declaration to Abraham, because He cannot lie;

"I will bless those who bless you, and I will curse him who curses you; and in you all the families of the earth shall be blessed" (Gen. 12:3).

But people or nations that seem to be doing the opposite are "blessed." God knows what He is doing.

A didactic study of God's patterns as revealed in the Bible shows a prophetic silver lining of His last days' agenda. When nations, people, families (especially those that serve God) are in any crisis, especially economic hardship (famine), God would usually raise prophets from among the same people. A prophet in this context is not the spooky, phony, "all-knowing" individual, who claims to know everything about your life. A prophet is simply a person who has been entrusted with God's mind and will for His people and who has been sent to declare it.

These prophets are usually ordinary people that have been chosen for whatever reason known to God Himself. They are usually not perfect, may not be eloquent, may be physically insipid or may not even be educated.

This is not implying that these seemingly human inadequacies are what qualify them, but to say that God still calls them in spite of them. The only thing that qualifies a person in the service of God is GRACE. In fact, God does not call those who think they are qualified, but He qualifies the chosen.

"(26)For you see your calling, brethren, that not many wise according to the flesh, not many mighty, not many noble, are called. (27)But God has chosen the foolish things of the world to put to shame the wise, and God has chosen the weak things of the world to put to shame the things which are mighty; (28)and the base things of the world and the things which

are despised God has chosen, and the things which are not, to bring to nothing the things that are, *(29)that no flesh should glory in His presence"* (1 Cor. 1:26-29).

A true prophet shows up with God's word and power in the middle of crisis, distress, pain or adversity and begins to declare the word of the Lord as he is moved by the Holy Spirit for those who dare to believe.

When and if you believe what the prophet is declaring over your life, then God begins to re-arrange certain things in the universe that would bring the physical reality or manifestation of what he has said.

GOD'S SYSTEM OF WEALTH TRANSFER

There is a consistent pattern God has used over and over again anytime He gets ready to re-arrange things in favor of His own especially in the area of wealth. It is called supernatural or prophetic wealth transfer.

In certain circles, it is believed that the imminent wealth transfer to the body of Christ is going to be totally spiritual. I agree, but to ignore the other sensible, intelligent, access method of it would be tantamount to a flagrant display of spiritual irresponsibility and buffoonery.

The basic fundamental tool God would use to stir this wave of wealth transfer is spiritual, which is the anointing, grace, favor, wisdom, endowment, power, the blessing and all of its other synonyms. The caveat is: even though the anointing is tangible and real in the realm of the unseen supernatural realm, it is not tangible and cannot be seen in the realm of the physical. So the "anointed" or "blessed" of the Lord must believe God for the

> *In certain circles, it is believed that the imminent wealth transfer to the body of Christ is going to be totally spiritual. I agree, but to ignore the other sensible, intelligent, access method of it would be tantamount to a flagrant display of spiritual irresponsibility and buffoonery.*

grace to make it available in the realm of the seen without being carnal or spooky, which involves a certain level of grace and skills. Jesus Christ was both supernatural and physical in His dealings with men. We too are supposed to be supernaturally natural and naturally supernatural. Our Lord had the uncanny ability to be spiritually connected to His

Father while relating in the real world with people where they were by downloading from the realm of the spirit the language they could understand, not just the language but also their various needs.

He traveled back and forth between the two realms at the same time with the speed of light. For example, don't you think Jesus had the anointing to stop hunger in the life of 5,000 people by just laying or waving his hands on them? Sure, He could have done that and they would not even remember food for days or months. However, He chose to connect to the realm of the spirit to download the required grace that was needed to multiply the physically insufficient supply of food. He was not going to permanently suspend the natural order of things to prove He was anointed. Prayer and singing will never replace food for the hungry nor will praise and worship quench a physical thirst. These are spiritual exercises that we should do regularly, but I believe God wants us to be like Jesus in translating these spiritual, intangible exercises into consumable, usable, physical realities to show forth the goodness of the Lord to a hopeless and dying world.

In the study of the supernatural feeding of these 5,000 people, I realized that Jesus did not only convert the spiritual into the physical; He also created a system for the physically manifested miracle to be effectively served. He gave the surplus food to the disciples who made the crowd sit fifty by fifty before serving them. Again, He alone could have served the food but would have probably taken days for Him to do that which would have caused Him physical exhaustion. The people He was trying to feed would have fainted before the food got to them. The disciples too would have been idle, which is probably one of the worst things that can happen to a man (being seen as irrelevant).

Jesus used the same principle of downloading the physical, natural, consumable, usable equivalent of the anointing when He turned water into wine (drinkable/consumable). He commanded a fish to vomit money (physical means of exchange) for His tax purpose to avoid embarrassment from the Roman government (an equivalent of IRS; Uncle Sam today).

Going back in history, you will see the same pattern being repeated again and again. If God did it many times, He will do it again on a larger and final scale in these last days. A lot of people have myopically thought that money will develop legs and walk supernaturally from the hands of the wicked (unsaved) into the hands of the righteous (born-again Christians). While that can happen supernaturally where you could go to sleep a pauper and wake up the following morning a millionaire, it is wise to stick to the consistent, ever-working principle that is predictable instead of living your life on chances. I would rather get involved with a predictable, Godly system, while expecting miracles rather than expect miracles while ignoring Godly principles. I would also rather be taught how to work miracles rather than be taught to be on the other side of the equation. The Bible justifies the wealth transfer proposition;

"...But the wealth of the sinner is stored up for the righteous" (Prov. 13:22).

An analytical study of this Scripture reveals so many instances of its predictability in the entire Bible. In the beginning, it may look like the wicked is winning, but in the end the wisdom of God would always triumph. I believe without any shadow of doubt that God's methodology for the transfer of wealth from the wicked (those who don't acknowledge God) to the righteous is going to be predicated on the same principle of being able to download from heaven or the realm of the spirit divine wisdom that is consumable, usable and physically tangible. If everything is going to be spiritual, some productions and exchange of goods and services would stop, thereby bringing the global economy to a precarious standstill. The beautiful thing is that God's children have an advantage that is firmly rooted on the grace of God. So, when they bring valuable service or product to the marketplace, with the consciousness of God's grace, everybody, including unbelievers, will have no choice but to purchase them. To just take their money "supernaturally" without an exchange would be stealing. Anybody who wants to be rich "supernaturally" without offering anything in return is only fit for the prison. This is so simple and yet millions of God's children all over the world still pray against the "spirit of poverty," run after "prophets" to break the "yoke of poverty" without asking God "what should I be offering?"

Let me make an audacious, controversial statement. Every member of the human race still operates in the general "blessing" that God released unto the first man, *"... And God blessed them..."* (Genesis 1:28). That word *"blessed"* is still active to some extent today on the earth in every human regardless of his background, color, and gender. The word of God will not return to Him void. That explains why members of the human race can procreate, learn and understand, make intelligent decisions, invent, and come up with concepts that bless people, sometimes without praying. No one is certain about the religious affiliations of some of the key players in today's digital inventions. Mark Zuckerberg of Facebook, Larry Page and the other Google guys, the late Steve Jobs of Apple, Jeff Bezos of Amazon etc, have all come up with inventions that everybody is using today. That's God's general blessing. But then the Christian has a double advantage because he does not just have the general or universal, Adamic blessing, he also has the Abrahamic covenant blessing, which is made available in Christ.

HISTORICAL PARALLELS

The following Bible heroes confirm the parallels of wealth transfer through product/service offerings.

Joseph: Joseph's gifts (dreams/ products and services) are spiritual, but he, like Jesus by God's grace was able to translate it into usable, consumable reality. He used his administrative gift to serve Potiphar and his gift of interpretation of dreams to explain the physical reality of Pharaoh's dreams. He also suggested a physically relevant, unambiguous proposal on how to solve the impending national calamity. The result was a wealth transfer from the national treasury of a heathen nation into Joseph's bank account. (He became the prime minister with a higher responsibility but also a higher remuneration and benefits).

Israel: When God decided to transfer the wicked's wealth unto the nation of Israel, they were asked to "borrow" jewelry, gold and other valuables from the Egyptians, an act of physical obedience and responsibility on their part. These items were theirs in the first place because they labored in the slave markets. Unfortunately, he who owns the slave also owns what the slave has. That was not going to be forever. God in His infinite wisdom drowned the enemies in the Red Sea. Of course, those borrowed items transferred to the Israelites, the original owners, until God asked for them at the construction of the tabernacle in the wilderness (Exodus 12:29-36).

David: 1 Samuel 16, 17; David's anointing service, in his father's house by prophet Samuel, was spiritual and supernatural but he converted it into usable, functional, physical reality when he fired a rock that snuffed life out of Goliath. The Philistines were captured as slaves after the death of their champion. Again, whoever owns the slave owns everything the slave has. All the bounties of the Philistines transferred into the treasury of Israel.

Solomon: The same principle applies to Solomon. Everything about his encounter with God at Gibeon was spiritual. There was no physical sign that God answered his request for knowledge and wisdom except the answer God gave in the affirmative. We begin to see the physical, consumable manifestation of his intangible wisdom when he resolved the squabbles between the two women who were trying to claim the living child. His fame spread abroad to other Kings and Queens, many of who didn't have covenant with God. They came with their riches to consult with Solomon not only because he could pray but because he could solve their problems. Their riches were exchanged for Solomon's wisdom (consulting) (2 Chron. 9:22-28). You will recall what the Scripture says in 1 Kings 10: 4-5.

> *"(4)And when the queen of Sheba had seen all the wisdom of Solomon, the house that he had built, (5)the food on his table, the seating of his servants, the service of his waiters and their apparel, his cupbearers, and his entryway by which he went up to the house of the LORD, there was no more spirit in her."*

God's impeccable, supernatural wisdom was upon Solomon but was invisible and intangible. It was Solomon's responsibility to translate it into what could be seen. *"…when the Queen of Sheba had seen Solomon's wisdom…"* His wisdom had been physically manifested into an excellent reality as seen in the beauty of his house, decent, healthy food, immaculate dress sense and the flawless organization and management of his domestic staff. The queen opened up her treasury and handsomely rewarded King Solomon for answering all her questions (solved her problems).

Jacob: This same concept comes to mind when you study the life of Jacob. He exchanged his delicious food for Esau's wealth transfer. What Esau legally transferred unknown to him was more than the title of "first born," but every benefit that came with it. Could that be the reason why Jacob prospered exceedingly? Isaac their father pronounced the "blessing" which was spiritual and unseen, but its tangibility was frequently utilized throughout Jacob's business life. From "nothing," he bargained for part equity ownership of Laban's livestock and dairy business after translating the blessing into its material reality in the realm of the physical for an exchange of his bargain. Laban's sons, like many unrealistic people today, accused Jacob of defrauding their father of his wealth. They should have asked their father if he was drugged when he accepted Jacob's proposal. They also forgot that Laban changed Jacob's salary ten times. Every covenant child of God is just one divine idea or witty invention away from a prophetic wealth transfer. So stop blaming people. In fact, I double dare you to ignore the devil and focus on Jesus and the benefits of redemption by walking closely with Him and you will begin to operate under an open heaven. The devil and demons are not your problems, they have been defeated; period.

The Broke Widow: The story of the hopeless widow who was so poor that her sons were used as collateral for her loans is a classic example of an intelligent, product-serving, wealth transfer. Prophet Elisha did not just "prophesy" on the pot of oil for multiplication but also functioned as a "teacher" by instructing her on what to do *"...Go, sell the oil and pay your debt; and you and your sons live on the rest* (2 Kings 4:7). She became an oil magnate in her community. The wealth of the people was exchanged for her oil.

The Parable of Dollars: In Matthew 25, the parable of dollar is an example of wealth transfer from the wicked to the righteous. Interestingly, the righteous in this context is only righteous because he is a meticulous, pragmatic, resourceful guy who knows how to maximize whatever he has been given. He gets more when the owner returns. The one who hides his resources like most Christians do today in the name of prayer, fasting and deliverance services is stripped of the little he has and given to the guy with plenty; wealth transfer.

The Jewish Community Today: It is amazing that the prophetic words that came on Abraham, the founding father of the Jewish race are still active today. Thousands of years after God declared the blessing on Abraham, his descendants are still enjoying that grace of God. Unlike many people, even though they believe the spiritual tangibility of the promise, they have learned like their predecessors that there has to be a real, physical system through which the blessing will flow and translate to its physical, usable, consumable relevance. Today, it is not uncommon to find the Jews in some of the most enterprising endeavors. They are so proud of their heritage. In *The Jewish Phenomenon*, Steven Silbiger writes, "For the Jews, wealth is a good thing, a worthy and respectable goal to strive toward. What's more, once you earn it, it is tragic to lose it. Judaism has never considered poverty a virtue. The first Jews were not poor, and that was good. The Jewish founding fathers: Abraham, Isaac, and Jacob were blessed with cattle and lands in abundance ..., with your financial house in order; it is easier to pursue your spiritual life." Also, Herbert Adams wrote in *Columbus and His Discovery of America*, "Not jewels, but Jews, were the real financial basis of the first expedition of Columbus." The following statistics about the present day Jews is staggering. Again, it is a testament to the efficacy of the immutability of God's nature. He cannot lie.

According to a study,

> Jews make up only 2 percent of the U.S. population yet 45 percent of the top forty of the Forbes 400 richest Americans are Jewish.

> One-third of all American multi-millionaires are Jewish.

> The percentage of Jewish households with income greater than 50,000 is double that of non-Jews.

> On the other hand, the percentage of Jewish households with income less than 20,000 is half that of the non-Jews.

> 20 percent of professors at leading universities are Jewish.

> 40 percent of partners in leading New York, D.C., law firms are Jewish.

> 25 percent of all American Nobel prize winners are Jewish.

> Notable names like Ralph Lauren, Michael Dell (Dell Computer), Albert Einstein, Barbara Walters and 50 percent of the twenty-five most powerful women were either Jews or had Jewish parents.

In addition, the following information provides a list of few people who were either born by Jewish parents or have paternal or maternal relationship with Jews.

Banking and Finance

Sandy Weill, former chairman and CEO of Citigroup

George Soros, Wall street investor and foreign currency speculator

Paul Warburg, chairman of Bank of America Manhattan company (Predecessor of Chase Manhattan Bank)

Technology

Mark Elliot Zuckerberg, CEO/President of Facebook

Steve Ballmer, CEO of Microsoft

Larry Page, co-founder of Google

Sergey Brin, co-founder of Google

Lawrence Ellison, founder of Oracle Corporation

Benjamin M. Rosen, founding investor and former chairman and CEO of Compaq

Television and Entertainment

Harry Cohn, founder of Columbia Pictures

Leonard Goldenson, President of ABC

Barry Diller, CEO of 20th Century fox

Michael Eisner, CEO of Disney

Adolph Zukor, founder of Paramount Pictures

Sam Warner, co-founder of Warner Brothers Studios

Carl Laemmle, founder of Universal Pictures

Jeff Zucker, NBC President

Fashion and Retail

Calvin Klein, founder and CEO of Calvin Klein

Levi Strauss, founder of Levi Strauss and Co clothing company

Kenneth Cole, founder of Kenneth Cole productions

Diane Von Furstenberg, founder and CEO of Diane Von Furstenberg

Isidor Straus, co-founder of Macy's department store

Julius Rosenwald, president and chairman of the board of Sears

Sol Price, founder of Price Club, (later merged with Costco)

Howard Schultz, founder, chairman and CEO of Starbucks coffee

Bernard Marcus, Co-founder of Home Depot

So, following the principle I have been addressing, wealth transfer continues even till today in the Jewish community. However, the beautiful thing is that you don't have to come from a natural Jewish heritage to actively participate in the blessing. Everyone who has a relationship with Christ is Abraham's seed, which is even more glorious.

"(13)Christ has redeemed us from the curse of the law, having become a curse for us (for it is written, "Cursed is everyone who hangs on a tree"), (14)that the blessing of Abraham might come upon the Gentiles in Christ Jesus, that we might receive the promise of the Spirit through faith" (Gal. 3:13-14).

What that means for you and I is that there are still many ideas untapped, many inventions, concepts, books, poems, songs, movies, games, sports, businesses etc. in the realm of the spirit. The prophets of God will continue to release God's word into your life. It is going to be your responsibility to believe God for wisdom and faith to translate or download the spiritual blessing in the heavenly places into this material world.

Even if you cannot invent new concepts or ideas, you can improve on old ones. You can help somebody re-package his idea. No prophetic word will ever come to pass on its own. There is always a collaboration of the prophetic instructions and its recipient.

> *The coming wealth transfer will reach its climax when the body of Christ conquers greed and gives generously to the funding of the kingdom of God. Otherwise, of what use is it going to be for God to transfer wealth from one wicked to another "wicked." Get ready! It's your moment.*

The coming wealth transfer will reach its climax when the body of Christ conquers greed and gives generously to the funding of the kingdom of God. Otherwise, of what use is it going to be for God to transfer wealth from one wicked to another "wicked." Get ready! It's your moment.

Study Guide

---

1. Study and do a didactic, analytical study of the following characters with your study group. Please remember to include these vital elements in your analysis.

   a. Their product or service

   b. The systems they put in place

   c. Their spiritual background and heritage

   d. The twenty-first century relevance of their products/services

       i.   Jacob

       ii.   Joseph

       iii.   David

       iv.   Solomon

       v.   Peter

       vi.   Paul

       vii.   Bezalel

       viii. Jesus Christ

Chapter 18

GETTING THE HORSE READY

The Power Factor

Everything referred to in the last chapters is our responsibility. In this chapter, I want to zero in on God's own responsibility. You will only exhaust yourself, if it is left to you to execute everything God intended for you without His help. The results will be frustration and despondency. However, when the grace of God rests on your own abilities, you will be supernaturally equipped to get the task done.

"Behold, I send the Promise of My Father upon you; but tarry in the city of Jerusalem until you are endued with power from on high" (Luke 24:49).

If you are not experiencing the power of God in your life to accomplish certain tasks, you are going to toil. The word "tarry" means "to wait." Jesus advised His disciples not to venture into any ministry work on their own strength because He knew they couldn't do anything meaningful without the anointing. This was what happened on the day of Pentecost when the disciples gathered together to wait on God in the upper room as instructed by Jesus. There is always the part every human being is supposed to play in the drama of purpose. We must not forget to let God play His own role too, which is more important.

"The horse is prepared for the day of battle, but deliverance is of the LORD" (Prov. 21:31).

You can stir up your gift, brand and market it, but you can only accomplish everything God planned for you in every area of life, through God's grace and His anointing. Your skills, talents, intelligence, networking, and relationships are all great, but there are many people who have all of those things and are still frustrated with life. They have great skills, and are well connected. They might have done everything they needed to do, but because of their inability to connect to the power of God, they're still despondent. Let's look at marriage for example. For you to experience bliss in marriage, you are required to act on God's instructions regarding it. In addition to that, you may need to buy books, CDs and DVDs in order to receive practical teachings and admonitions from those with greater insights.

However, do you know anyone who bought CDs, read books, went to seminars, and still had a bad marriage? I bet you do. Many couples really struggle hard to make their marriages work but sadly, the harder they try, the worse things become. This is because the power factor is missing or perhaps the foundation is faulty. Also, do you know people who have done every single thing they were supposed to do to maintain a good healthy habit?

They eat right, exercise, and go on vacations regularly yet they have health issues. They have done everything health specialists have recommended to them but they're still weak and sickly, because of the lack of the power factor.

Do you also know people who are still struggling in the realm of their finance, even though they have done everything they can possibly do? They are hard working, and also give sacrificially from their income.

They spend within their budget, but they're still overwhelmed with debts, and still struggling because of their inability to connect to the grace factor and the anointing of the Holy Ghost.

CONNECTING TO THE SUPERNATURAL

"It shall come to pass in that day that his burden will be taken away from your shoulder, and his yoke from your neck, and the yoke will be destroyed because of the anointing oil" (Isa. 10:27).

No matter how gifted you are, if you lack the grace of God, you will still struggle in life, moving around in circles. That is not God's will though, because He wants to be involved in your life so that you will not brag in your ability and think you have done everything through your hard work and human intellect only.

The Scripture in reference is one of my favorite Scriptures. One of my greatest temptations is over-reliance on my abilities and strategies. I believe in working around the clock and sometimes have the tendency to unconsciously relegate the grace factor to the background. Maybe you are like one of those who believe they can do it all. They have the energy and strength, are brilliant and well connected, but even with all these, they cannot go far without God's power.

The Scripture also shows the correlation between developing your skills and doing what you are supposed to do after which you depend on the grace of God to accomplish it. One of the challenges in the body of Christ today is the inability to strike a balance between extremes. There are some people who believe that you are not supposed to do anything at all, because they believe God will do everything.

> *There are some people who believe that you are not supposed to do anything at all, because they believe God will do everything. They depend solely on the anointing, but this is false teaching. There are also some who believe that they can do everything on their own while ignoring the factor of grace. This is humanism (that man is his own god). This is also false.*

They depend solely on the anointing, but this is false teaching. There are also some who believe that they can do everything on their own while ignoring the factor of grace. This is humanism (that man is his own god). This is also false. The truth is, you are required to do your part, and believe God for the release of His power for what you cannot do. I have since learned from Kenneth E. Hagin, who, in his book *The Believer's Authority*, advises that the wise thing to do is to have "a middle of the road approach on controversial issues of life"

For instance, an un-anointed, professional motivational speaker can counsel you and say you can do anything you imagine, to a point that they over glorify your mind and knock out the grace factor. For this reason, Paul said in the epistle;

> "[4]*And my speech and my preaching were not with persuasive words of human wisdom, but in demonstration of the Spirit and of power, [5]that your faith should not be in the wisdom of men but in the power of God* (1 Cor. 2:4-5).

We need to get to the place of total surrender to God where we give everything to Him. Horses are very strong animals with special ability to run long distances without getting tired. They hardly get sick, because of their strong immune system.

This explains why certain vehicles or electrical appliances are calibrated in horse power to explain their strength and reliability. Skills, talents and abilities are great, especially when they are developed and that refers to the preparation which horses go through. The Bible does not say horses should not be prepared, but it implies that after all is done, safety is of the Lord.

My stepbrother who was one of the best medical students in his class was "unintelligent" while in elementary school. There was no hope for him. But my other stepbrother was very brilliant; he was being praised like the person that would probably turn out the best. By the time both got to high school, there was a reverse order of their abilities, the one that was considered not smart enough exceptionally did very well. When the final result was released, the "unintelligent" boy scored A in every course, and went on to study medicine becoming one of the foremost pathologists. This is why you cannot write off anybody, especially if that person has a connection with the supernatural wisdom of God. This wisdom can change a man overnight. Look at the story of Joseph for example; even though he developed his skills, it was God's surpassing intelligence that eventually promoted him. Was it his skills that made him become the prime minister? Yes, his skills were part of it, but it had more to do with the referral from the butler orchestrated by God. Somebody had to mention his name to the king. Two years earlier the butler forgot, but when the appointed time came, he remembered. Now the question is, who reminded him? God of course.

> *Look at the story of Joseph for example; even though he developed his skills, it was God's surpassing intelligence that eventually promoted him.*

He is the only one that can connect you to the throne. Success is not just about skills alone, it was not just skills that brought President Barrack Obama to the white house. Grace was the main thing. Thank God for his skills, but above all thank God for His grace. I believe very strongly in my heart that God Himself was the one who arranged certain chain of events that finally moved him to where he was at the right time, at the right place. It was grace that gave him the right words to speak and made the right people to be there at that point in time. They were not just coincidences. Even if you believe in coincidences, who orchestrates them? The answer is, the Almighty God.

Everybody has something in them for God to use. However, there are some things you need to present to God for Him to anoint or bless. All you need to do is lay them down. The problem with so many of us today is that we hold on so tenaciously to what we have.

We are so attached to certain things that we have turned them into idols. Don't idolize anything God has given to you. Lay it down. The next chapter elaborates on this point.

Study Guide

---

1. Identify three things you are currently doing without the anointing (power of God).

    a.

    b.

    c.

2. Which gift or ability have you consecrated to the Lord?

    a.

    b.

    c.

3. Which of your gifts or abilities do you engage with grace?

    _____

    _____

    _____

4. How often do you pray, fast and meditate on God's word for the purpose of spiritually energizing your core gift?

5. What type of spiritual conferences do you attend, and how often?

6. What types of books, journals, magazines, and other resources do you study to sharpen your gifts?

Chapter 19

ENGAGING YOUR ASSETS

Laying Down Your Gift at the Feet of the Giver

For every recipient of God's miracle, especially in the area of finance, God will always give them something to start with. Then at some point, they will have to lay them down. These principles run throughout the entire Scriptures. For instance, God provided food for the widow of Zarephath because He gives bread to the eater and seed to the sower. As recorded in the Bible, Prophet Elijah went to the widow's house and requested for the last portion of her food (1 Kings 17). The confirmation of a true prophet is that whatever he says will come to pass. Prophet Elijah painted the picture of an abundant future for that woman; that while others were going to die in the famine, the woman and her son would live.

When she saw hope in the words of the prophet, she was inspired to give. Also, the widow whose husband left with so much debts to the point that the debtors came around to collect their money is a case in point. She was so desperate that she used her son as collateral for the loan. When asked what she had in the house, her reply was that she had nothing.

"So Elisha said to her, What shall I do for you? Tell me, what do you have in the house? And she said, Your maidservant has nothing in the house but a jar of oil" (2 Kings 4:2).

The prophet assured her that it was the exact same thing God would anoint for her deliverance. The anointing of God came upon that pot of oil and even after paying off her debts, still had left over. All David had was a sling and a rock, but the anointing of God came upon him and that was all he needed to bring Goliath down. Unknown to David, God had been preparing him at the back of the desert for his battle with Goliath. On seeing him, he said, *"...You come to me with a sword, with a spear, and with a javelin. But I come to you in the name of the LORD of hosts, the God of the armies of Israel, whom you have defied"* (1 Sam. 17:4-5).

This is a caution for most of us who get carried away into developing our skills to a point that we forget the Giver of the gift. Please don't make that mistake. I believe the power from God, the Giver of the anointing, rested on David's rock that liquidated the fake giant.

> *When God's grace comes on a thing, there will be multiplication and expansion. You don't know how big your resources, ability or gift can become until you lay it down at the feet of the Giver.*

The little boy who attended the crusade of Jesus in the wilderness laid down his lunch, which his mother probably packed for him. Jesus prayed over the physically insufficient supply and as they began breaking the bread, it began to supernaturally multiply. Everything that you bring to God will multiply. When God's grace comes on a thing, there will be multiplication and expansion. You don't know how big your resources, ability or gift can become until you lay it down at the feet of the Giver. It seems God cannot do anything supernatural for human beings until they have laid down something. For example, God asked Moses to lay down the rod in his hands, so that He could use it.

The rod of Moses became a snake after he cast it on the ground from which he fled. God told Moses to put forth his hand and take the snake by the tail which became a rod in his hand. For a long time I did not understand that. Why would God tell somebody to hold a snake by the tail? The most intelligent and safe place to hold a snake is the neck, right?

The reason is because God wanted Moses to put his trust in Him. Also, Moses was being symbolically reminded of what happened in the Garden of Eden because God already announced that the seed of the woman will bruise the head of the serpent.

Moses did not need to grab the snake (the devil) by the head because the head of the snake had already been bruised spiritually. Also, even with the gifts and talents that God has given to man, there's still the element of the fallen nature. It is only when the anointing of the Holy Ghost comes on them that they are purified. The rod of Moses which was symbolic of his abilities and resources still had the element of the fallen nature. The same rod (gift) was transformed into a snake. Moses was instructed to take the snake by the tail and it turned to rod. Some theologians say that the abilities, gifts, and resources that we have today contain certain elements of serpentine influences; an imperfect system, deceits, perversion and when we lay them down like Moses did the rod, they go through a process of purification.

They may not be far from the truth which could probably explain the reasons why certain gifted, talented people would use their gifts to do so well in life but the same gifts would bring them down. That could also explain why historically, most Emperors with magnificent empires finally fell and kissed the dust. Even Hollywood is churning out highly gifted young people every now and then, but some become villains within a short period of stardom through illicit sex, perversion, drug abuse, imprisonment etc. Maybe their gifts need Holy Ghost cleansing.

> *Some theologians say that the abilities, gifts, and resources that we have today contain certain elements of serpentine influences; an imperfect system, deceits, perversion and when we lay them down like Moses did the rod, they go through a process of purification.*

Some people still struggle with selfishness, bitterness and many other impurities, but God wants His power to come upon those giftings until they get purified. He wants to rid us of everything that has to do with fear and every characteristic of the fallen man. Moses did not know that what he was holding had an element of the fallen nature in it.

From that moment on, Moses realized that the rod he was holding was not an ordinary rod. When it was in his hands, it was the rod of Moses, but when God told him to cast it down at His instruction, it became the rod of God. Throughout Moses' life, he used that rod many times to perform miracles. It was the same rod that he used to strike the Red Sea to part ways for the children of Israel to walk through.

Sometimes you may not know the potential of your ability and gift until the power of God comes on it. When the grace of God comes on your abilities, you will use them perfectly well. Why is it that some people will do certain things with ease, and some people will toil to do the same thing? The answer lies in the grace factor.

"(1)So it was, as the multitude pressed about Him to hear the word of God, that He stood by the Lake of Gennesaret, (2)and saw two boats standing by the lake; but the fishermen had gone from them and were washing their nets. (3)Then He got into one of the boats, which was Simon's, and asked him to put out a little from the land. And He sat down and taught the multitudes from the boat. (4) When He had stopped speaking, He said to Simon, "Launch out into the deep and let down your nets for a catch" (Luke 5:1-4).

When fishermen wash their nets, it signifies they have closed for the day. That was exactly what Peter and his business partners were doing when Jesus came to the scene. Peter was a professional fisherman, who was skillful and gifted in the art of fishing. But on a particular day his skills and gift failed him, so he toiled all night and caught nothing. May you not lack grace in whatever you are called to do. At Jesus' instruction, Peter had to lay down his boat for Him to use. God is asking you to lay down your instrument, platform, gifts and talents at His feet.

You can't effectively dispense on your own, the horse is prepared for the day of battle, but don't forget, safety is of the Lord. In verse four, when Jesus finished preaching His sermon, He said to Simon, *"let down your NETS."* The obedience of Peter was not complete; but thank God for mercy because Peter only let down his NET, and this was why the net was breaking.

God knew that one net would not be enough to contain the kind of harvest that was on its way. I think Peter's reluctance was due to his frustration. Maybe you have been in situations where you had to obey God reluctantly and half heartedly. The Scripture says their net broke. God is going to give you a harvest that you cannot handle alone. You will need partners.

SUPERNATURAL SPEED

If you are familiar with the story of Elijah and King Ahab in 1 Kings19, you'll find out that the two were in a race to Jezreel shortly before a torrential rain hit the planet after three years of devastating drought that brought untold famine and hardship on the people. In the race to Jezreel, the only difference between King Ahab and Elijah was the anointing of God. The king depended on his horse; he depended on his natural strength and abilities, his gifts, and his preparations while Elijah depended on the power of God. He depended on his God-given prophetic anointing that he had developed and sharpened over the years. The Bible says Elijah outran the man on the horseback. According to Bible scholars, the distance that Elijah ran was between fifteen and twenty miles. As a result of the grace and power of God on his life, Elijah out ran the king's chariots. The distance between you and your colleagues now does not matter. When the power of God comes on you, it does not matter how far they've gone. Hannah gave birth to Samuel after years of waiting.

Penninah, her rival, was mocking her before she gave birth; but when Samuel came to the scene, Bible records show that Samuel did so many exploits for God to a point that he wrote two bestselling books that have never gone out of print, entitled *First and Second Samuel*. Elizabeth gave birth to John the Baptist after years of barrenness, and he became the forerunner of the Savior. So the horse is prepared for the day of battle, but safety is of the Lord.

The word "Prepare" in Hebrew is "qum." Which means "to stand firm" and "to be established." It means "to be steadfast, faithful, strong and reliable." It means "to be determined." The word "prepare" means "to set up and be sure." It means "to build or rebuild, to make ready, or to be set in order." Actually, "prepare" is a military terminology that is used in the Hebrew culture to refer to stages of combat ready, rigorous training.

It refers to the point when you say "I'm now ready for anything." This is the time when you have read for an exam and after hours of studying, you have that sense of security that you will be successful.

Many people get to this stage in their fifties and sixties when they have worked all their lives, invested in real estate, stocks and other ventures, and are ready for retirement. This stage is what the Bible calls "kul." In Hebrew, it means you are formed, established and ready to cruise. Unfortunately, as fulfilling and rewarding this season appears to be superficially, it is still dangerous without God's enablement. Your permanent security is only guaranteed in God.

For example, many establishments have crumbled over the years when they got to this stage. Remember Enron, The Leman Brothers and Merrill Lynch, some of them had to be rescued by tax payers' money. The Roman Empire was so great, but it collapsed. The Babylonian Empire was also colossal, but it too disintegrated; likewise the temple of Solomon, with all its magnificence. I look at certain pastors who brag and boast in how many buildings they have and I shake my head. How many buildings did Jesus erect when He was alive? None. He did not have to be defined by any of those.

I don't have anything against buildings, as long as they are serving the purpose of God and blessing humanity. Check this out, two thousand years after the death of Jesus Christ, Christianity remains the most powerful force on earth, without Jesus erecting a single building.

By the time my work on earth is done, if the Lord tarries, the legacy I want to leave behind are not necessarily just going to be buildings, but also books. Books about God's grace through the cross in different formats depending on the available technology at the time that people will be reading, 400-1,000 years or more after I am gone. Apostle Peter and Paul and all the other apostles who wrote books left a legacy that is beyond them. We're still reading about them several years after they have gone. That is what it means to reach the level of being satisfied after doing all that is required with your gifts through divine empowerment.

Study Guide

---

1. If you were to lay down a gift at God's feet now, what will it be and are you willing?

2. Discuss with your accountability partner or study group three people in the Bible who laid down their resources for God's use.
   a.
   b.
   c.

3. Discuss three benefits of question two above.
   a.
   b.
   c.

4. Bible scholars believed that our raw gifts in their very best without God have elements of serpentine nature. Discuss this with your group.

5. "The horse is prepared for the day of battle, but safety is of the Lord." Discuss this Bible verse in relation to using your gift without God's grace.

6. Discuss with your study group why a lot of gifted people usually come crashing down after some level of success.

7. What are the pro-active systems you have put in place to overcome greed? Discuss three of them with your group.
   a.
   b.
   c.

8. If you do not have any, what are your plans? Write them down and discuss with your accountability partner.
   a.
   b.
   c.

Part Five

THE APOCALYPSE

Chapter 20

KINGDOMS TAKEOVER

The Dominion Mandate

The last words of any prodigious man are always very important to him because of many reasons:

Those words are usually the first on his priority list.

He does not seem to have much time left.

He would probably want those words to linger in the memory of his loved ones forever.

Those who have been privileged to hear the last words of their aged, dying parents consider it one of the greatest honors of their life. In certain cultures, it is perceived as a double tragedy when old people die without being able to say their last words to their children.

Little wonder therefore, that the old patriarchs, Abraham, Isaac, Jacob and the others will always gather their children together and talk to them before they passed on, and their last words were usually prophetic.

"(1)And Jacob called his sons and said, "Gather together, that I may tell you what shall befall you in the last days: (2)"Gather together and hear, you sons of Jacob, and listen to Israel your father…" (Gen. 49:1-2).

Also, Jesus Christ our Lord and Savior before He went into glory gave us one of the most important instructions of all (His last words).

"(18)And Jesus came and spoke to them, saying, "All authority has been given to Me in heaven and on earth. (19)Go therefore and make disciples of all the nations, baptizing them in the name of the Father and of the Son and of the Holy Spirit, (20)teaching them to observe all things that I

have commanded you; and lo, I am with you always, even to the end of the age." Amen. (Matt. 28:18-20)

That does not sound to me like "building empires." Church buildings and services are only relevant to the degree of the impartation the people are receiving to disciple the nations, which in this context could be their spheres of influence. Some people may never pastor a church or get involved in any of the five-fold public ministry, but they can help influence a whole culture where God has planted them such as schools, hospitals, offices etc. In fact, there has been a rise in the popularity of the kingdom message and marketplace Christianity in recent times.

I must confess to you that I had not always understood the great commission as entailing discipling the nations from the perspective of training and releasing people into the marketplace. My understanding, just like a vast majority of Christians, had been limited to preaching the gospel of salvation, which entails being born again; filled with the Holy Spirit; being healed and delivered. These are all great, and we have done them excellently, but I believe like others who received this revelation before me that everything we have done so far is the foundation for discipling the nations. However, because revelation is progressive, my objective in this book is not to castigate or cast aspersions on the older generation of leaders who probably just focused on the message of salvation. They did their best through the measure of God's grace on their lives to pave the way for us.

A FRESH MOVE

It is my belief that the nations of the earth would soon begin to practically experience the impact of God's grace in every endeavor. Several years ago, I began to feel some "uneasiness" that God had called me to stir up a "revolution." I was meditating on Jesus' temptation account in Luke 4 when suddenly a revelation hit me like a thunderstorm. For the first time, I saw the heart of Jesus for the earth. The devil suggested to Him to bow down and worship him, and all the kingdoms of this world and their glory (splendor) would be His since Adam legally gave them to the devil. First of all, I noticed that Jesus did not contest the claim that what the devil said was heretic. Heresy, you must understand is not a complete lie but a mixture of lies and truths. Even though the devil cannot tell the truth (John 8:44), he heretically referred to the lease agreement he signed with Adam to have control of the earth. However, he did not know that the reason for Jesus' coming was to legally take it back from him through God's eternal wisdom. Jesus would have to go through His passion to pay the required price for our redemption. Therefore, He did not have to bow down to Satan. Instead, He voluntarily laid down His life.

I was blown away to see that the kingdoms of this world have "glory" which also means wealth or influence. Just take a good look into the various industries and the major players at the center stage, and this will give you an idea of how influential they are. The more I studied it, the more lonely I became (I felt nobody would understand me).

> *I was blown away to see that the kingdoms of this world have "glory" which also means wealth or influence. Just take a good look into the various industries and the major players at the center stage, and this will give you an idea of how influential they are.*

Then, I met my good friend, Pastor Sunday Adelaja who practically lives this revelation in Europe using these principles. We hosted him and his team from Ukraine in our Church and the revelation God gave me went to another level. I felt humbled like Elijah who thought he was the only prophet who had not bowed to Baal.

Then came Dr. Myles Munroe's revelation of the kingdom message that I devoured. God began to confirm this message by showing me my role in this project as He begins to lead me to the resources of other people who have been doing this for a longer time; people like Loren Cunningham of Youth with a Mission, the late Dr. Bill Bright of Campus Crusade (both received this revelation in 1975) and recently, Johnny Enlow, whose book *The Seven Mountain Prophecy* was a tremendous blessing to me. Even though the message and the premise are the same, there are a few variations in the semantics and style.

When I saw this revelation in Luke 4, I believe there could be 7 kingdoms that must be taken. Loren Cunningham called them "7 spheres of influence"; Johnny Enlow called them "7 mountains." I believe the three synonyms can be used interchangeably without fussing over semantic applications. The preference of the word you have chosen is not as important as the understanding of your responsibility in taking over these areas by establishing the reign of Christ.

"...the kingdoms of this world have become the kingdoms of our Lord and of His Christ, and He shall reign forever and ever!" (Revelation 11:15)

Again, the word of God has both present and futuristic dimensions and interpretations. Even though this Scripture is primarily referring to future events, its relevance to the present must be contextually understood.

Again, I want to appreciate Loren Cunningham, Bill Bright, Myles Munroe, Sunday Adelaja, Francis Schaeffer, and Johnny Enlow for their faithfulness in spreading this message. These people have been instrumental in taking away my "loneliness" when I did not know that there were other people with similar revelation.

My purpose here is not to write another detailed book explaining the different spheres of influence. I believe there are good books out there on the subject. My objective by the special grace of God is to provide individual strategies to get involved in taking over these kingdoms as we establish the kingdom of God through Christ. I will therefore outline these kingdoms and their relevance today and how you can leverage your gifts in taking over one or two of them for the glory of God. They are:

Family

Religion

Education

Politics/Government

Media

Entertainment (Arts, Sports)

Business

1. THE KINGDOM OF FAMILY

The word "kingdom" also means "domain, reign, or influence." These spheres, kingdoms or mountains have an objective to influence people.

Traditionally, the family unit is made up of the husband (father), the wife (mother) and the children. For a family to function effectively and according to God's design, five types of love must co-exist.

Table 4

FIVE TYPES OF LOVE	
Agape	God's own kind of love that is sacrificial, selfless and Christ centered.
Platonic	An innocent, no string attached type of love that is pure.
Erotic	Even though it has a negative, sensual connotative sense, it is nonetheless needed in marriage because you must be sexually attracted to your spouse.
Conjugal	This type of love exists between husband and wife for the purpose of getting married, and staying married.
Filial	There must be family love existing between husband, wife, and the children. When it is mutual, it is filial.

So what the evil spirit in charge of the family kingdom has sought to do is to turn everything about family values upside down. Anytime you read or hear about negative statistics regarding homes/family such as divorce rates, homosexuality, incestuous lifestyle, bestiality and other perversions, there is always a spiritual influence. Because of the lack of so many anointed, informed people serving the Lord in this arena, what we have is a bunch of dysfunctional families where children are raised in abusive environments and the results are inadequate self-image, and other psychological disorders, which could snowball into other violence and crimes.

If you are always being stirred up on anything that has to do with relationship or family and your core gift fits in, could it be that God is sending you to this mountain to teach parents how to raise their children in an atmosphere of love, affirmation, prayer and Godly discipline? Trust me; you will be in high demand in these last days because there are a whole lot of frustrated families out there. You can learn more from my book, *Towards A Purposeful Marriage*.

2. THE KINGDOM OF RELIGION

According to Wikipedia, an on-line free encyclopedia, statistics reveal that the world is presently about 6.8 billion people in population (now 7 billion according to a recent CNN report). More than 2.1 billion are Christians which include Charismatic/Pentecostal, Roman Catholics and Evangelicals. Islam is about 1.2 billion, Hinduism accounts for 900 million while Buddhism is over 300 million. There are other religions founded in occultism in Africa that account for over 100 million people. Thank God though, we are making progress, but we must not rest on our oars. Recent surveys reveal that:

90 percent of people in the marketplace believe in God and Christ

75 percent believe that there is a mix of their work and faith in Christ

More than 70 percent believe that they have found their purpose in life because of their faith in Christ

More than fifty-six million Bible believing Christians are working in the marketplace

About 90 percent of church members globally believe they have not been adequately informed or trained to be relevant in their spheres of influence

In 2005, there were 2 billion Christians in the world, an increase of 140 million from 1.8 billion in 2000. The increase in the Christian population is growing at a slightly higher rate than the world population; 1.3 percent per year, when the total world population increased by 1.2 percent. The Christian population in Asia and Africa had the highest growth with 2.6 percent and 2.4 percent, respectively, but the Christian population is declining in Europe.

Although the number of Muslims and Hindus; 1.31 billion Muslims and 870 million Hindus are less than Christians, the Muslim population has grown at a rate of 1.9 percent per year and the Hindu population has grown at a rate of 1.5 percent per year; however, charismatic Christianity and independent churches are growing at the fastest rate, 2.4 percent per year.

Karl Marx said "religion is the opium of the masses." He was wrong if he was implying that God cannot satisfy. He was right if his definition of religion without the true God is futile.

Religion is an attempt to relate with God while Christ is the way to relate with God in an acceptable manner. *"Jesus said to him, 'I am the way, the truth, and the life. No one comes to the Father except through Me'"* (John 14:6).

If you are called into this sphere of influence, you must be very sure of your exact, specific role. The body of Christ (the universal church) has been called to be the salt of the earth and the light of the world, and should be mobilized by the five-fold public ascension ministry gift.

" *(9)Now this, "He ascended"—what does it mean but that He also first descended into the lower parts of the earth? (10)He who descended is also the One who ascended far above all the heavens, that He might fill all things. (11)And He Himself gave some to be apostles, some prophets, some evangelists, and some pastors and teachers"* (Ephesians 4:9-11).

Just like the other kingdoms, there are many sub groups and derivatives of the main gifts that individual members of the body could function in effectively. Such ministries include helps, government, and administration with their variations. You need to stay in your lane and faithfully do whatever God has called you to do with excitement, commitment and excellence.

The church is advancing globally like an army like never before through the power of the Holy Spirit.

3. THE KINGDOM OF EDUCATION

The impact of education in the acculturation of a people or society cannot be ignored. Anyone who trivializes the significance of education is simply naïve. Education in this context generally refers to accumulation of knowledge in certain areas which can be formal, informal or both.

Ancient civilizations such as Greece, Babylon, Rome and other empires used the power of education to influence people and to change their thinking patterns. Some of their impacts are still being felt today. Some of the philosophies that have been adopted in our educational and political systems were propounded by people who are long dead and gone. For instance, democracy, a system of government modified by the United States was coined and developed by Aristotle and Plato, two Greek philosophers. The original Greek word is *democratia*.

The whole world today is clamoring for a government that would allow people to participate in the electoral process. The present skirmish in the Middle East is a classical example of an innate desire in every member of the human race to live a decent life like normal human beings without any form of repression or oppression. People can only be subjugated for so long. After a while, the God-given mandate of dominion in them will be stirred up, sometimes in a negative sense that could lead to a bloody revolution. We will likely see more of these revolutions in that region if their leaders still want to live in the past.

However, as useful, desirable and as legitimate proper education can be, it can at best be described as an attempt by man to get back to God. Man did not need to go to any university in the Garden of Eden to acquire education before he could be considered intelligent. It was not necessary. Adam named all the animals through God's intuition without being taught how to read or write. He and his wife had the best of times and "civilization" before the fall without any education. Our educational systems today in their best state will still never be compared to the atmosphere in the Garden before the fall. Man's attempt to educate himself is still part of the repercussion and consequences of the fall. Even though human beings have been redeemed from the curse of the fall potentially, our final and total redemption of all things will become a reality at the close of the age. Until then, it is going to be the responsibility of an individual child of God to believe God for the best for him or herself by faith in certain arenas of life.

> *Our educational systems today in their best state will still never be compared to the atmosphere in the Garden before the fall. Man's attempt to educate himself is still part of the repercussion and consequences of the fall.*

I am not by any means inferring that getting a good education is sinful; far from it. What I am insinuating is that the present, global educational system is a grandiose display of a fallen system. It is Babylon. Babylon metaphorically refers to an attempt to achieve success without a loving God. The word "Babylon" according to Bible Scholars is from the word "Babel" which means "confusion" or "scatter," sound familiar? The builders of the Tower of Babel had two main objectives. First, they were building a tower without God and second, they wanted to make a name for themselves. Does that sound like some of the things you see around today also? The Babylonian empire may no longer be physically present, but its spirit is every where. It too will collapse. The global economic crisis and the international impending disaster on those who have abandoned God is inevitable. The United States of America, the greatest country on earth is presently in the middle of a national debt debacle. Could this be a clarion call for the US to return back to the God of the Bible? Yes, I believe she will. America shall be saved. Maybe after a period of a purge that will soon shake the nations, then a Joseph generation will arise from the church that will fix the system through a divine download of witty ideas from heaven that will crack the confusing codes of political, social and economic doldrums.

Remember Nebuchadnezzar, the king of Babylon was banished into the jungle to feed with animals because of his arrogant ranting of his majesty without God. This is what "Greatness" without God is designed to achieve. Arrogance.

You see, humanistic, man-made education without God in its best form is a carnal attempt to interpret God's eternal words and values. The truth is, there is not a single branch of knowledge today that does not have a direct or indirect foundation in the Bible; medicine, engineering, pharmacy, real estate, law, accounting, journalism, banking, finance, to mention a few.

I strongly believe that our current educational system is a distortion of God's original plan; His Knowledge. That is why the word "secular" has been used to refer to anything that is humanistic or "unholy" in Christian circles. We use this term loosely to refer to anything that is seen as not fully representing God. Secular Television, Secular Radio, Secular Education, Secular Society etc. However, that wasn't meant to be in the first place because God owns everything. Things we call secular have become perverted and bastardized because of the fall of man. Otherwise the term would not have been necessary in the first place.

Historically, Christians established the first set of schools in America including the public school founded by John Cotton, a puritan minister. That was in 1635. Also, Harvard, Yale, Princeton and many of the oldest universities in America were all founded on Christian principles.

Even the prison system was originally established by the Presbyterian Church. The vision was to withdraw individuals violating the laws of the land from the civil society into a solitary place where they could be rehabilitated through God's word. The objective was hijacked by the government and turned into a humanistic, prison system that we see today. As a result of a lack of focus of succeeding generations and the carelessness of the church who did not understand the contextual difference between being worldly or being in the world, the god of this world, satan, put his foot in the system and began to plant people who eroded the original vision. Some of the so-called Secular Schools and hospitals all around the world were founded by Bible-believing missionaries. Today, majority of them if they are still existing are shadows of their past. They must be taken back.

I strongly advise children and parents alike to carefully and prayerfully choose to read courses that are related to their main giftings in these kingdoms. It is imperative for you to know your calling before choosing your course of study at the university. This will help you avoid wasting time and shorten your learning curves. I am eternally grateful to God for allowing me to study English language and Literature and a couple of minor courses in communications and journalism, even when I did not know why. Now I know.

Like other Kingdoms, education also has some sub-divisions and several derivatives.

4. KINGDOM OF POLITICS/GOVERNMENT

The kingdom of politics is very strategic because of its influence on the other kingdoms which explains why it is a do or die affair in certain countries. Some rulers in developing nations would rather die in power than relinquish it. It is like they seem to be in control of the soul of their nations. They could enact laws or make legislations, decree certain laws that could make or mar the efficiency of other spheres.

The individual called to this kingdom must be covered with prayer at all times in addition to being a true disciple of Jesus Christ. Putting a weak, terrible person in charge will only get little or no result. Any attempt to change a physical person in a place that is under the control of certain negative spiritual influence will be a waste of time.

The influencing demonic forces must be put under pressure through intercession and prayer of faith.

The caveat to that is to pray for an "upright, honest" individual who may not even be born again. Read this interesting passage from Paul to corroborate this point.

" *(1)Let every soul be subject to the governing authorities. For there is no authority except from God, and the authorities that exist are appointed by God. (2)Therefore whoever resists the authority resists the ordinance of God, and those who resist will bring judgment on themselves. (3)For rulers are not a terror to good works, but to evil. Do you want to be unafraid of the authority? Do what is good, and you will have praise from the same. (4) For he is God's minister to you for good. But if you do evil, be afraid; for he does not bear the sword in vain; for he is God's minister, an avenger to execute wrath on him who practices evil"* (Rom. 13:1-4).

The best approach though is for believers to get involved in politics and governments. If you are sensing the call of God upon your life for this mountain or kingdom, you need to start putting your strategies together with prayer, fasting and the word. The kingdom of politics or government also has its many sub-categories and sub-divisions.

5. THE KINGDOM OF MEDIA

The media is becoming more powerful and sophisticated than ever. Stories that would take days or even weeks to go around are disseminated in seconds across the planet. Certain means of communication like snail mail are now becoming irrelevant because of the power of digital media.

I do not think anybody; regardless of their gift can make a more meaningful, global impact without a creative engagement of one or two media outlets. The world indeed has become a global village. Traditional television and radio stations are now establishing their online divisions because of the power of the internet (no wonder the devil is called the prince of the air). Getting on the TV, radio or being a columnist in a famous, recognized newspaper automatically confers on you the title of an expert in your field, which is why the world is becoming celeb-crazy. Can you imagine the "celeb status" and using it to advance the kingdom of God?

If you are called to invade the media kingdom, endeavor to be planted in the media organizations with the most influence in your country of residence. Or better still you could believe God to start your own network like TBN, Daystar, The Church Channel, The Word Network, God TV, Gospel Channel etc. You have a much better advantage if you own because you are part of the decision making body that determines what gets on air unlike just being a puppet of some faceless mafias who just appear at certain times of the day to spill out what the boss wants into the atmosphere who in most cases is probably under demonic control.

The media can incite a revolution, they can topple governments, they can run people like robots which could be one of the reasons why my professor said while alluding to a slogan in journalism "the pen is mightier than the sword."

We need Holy Spirit filled, faith igniting, blood washed, fear destroying media people that will inject some hope in their writings or fill the air waves with faith as the case may be.

If you are a gifted communicator either in speaking, writing or both, you need to start praying for the strategies God will give you to invade this kingdom and turn it around for God.

6. THE KINGDOM OF ENTERTAINMENT (ARTS, SPORTS)

The kingdom of entertainment is in the vanguard of sabotaging the destinies of young people because of its immense influence on them. This Kingdom includes sports, entertainment such as movies, dance, music and fashion. The deal is, the devil is not a creator, he can only distort what has been created by God to make it look ungodly. That's why well-meaning Christians ignorantly think that the entertainment industry is a no go area, but the devil is a liar.

A good contextual study of the Holy Bible reveals that God is excellent and He delights in creativity and the arts. In fact, He displayed His artistic prowess when He molded Adam from the clay. Bible historians believe that the history of drama (also now known as movies) actually started in the church where playwrights like William Shakespeare and others used the church buildings to perform. It is also said that drama or movie and the church have a lot of similarities. The preacher could represent the actor, the platform the stage, the sanctuary, the theater and the congregation, the audience.

On one occasion, the disciples of Jesus returned from the field and were excited at how demons bowed to them and the Bible says, *"In that hour Jesus rejoiced in the Spirit ... "* (Luke 10:21). This statement in the original Greek is translated "...and Jesus did a few dance steps..." Jesus was a great dancer who had a social life. His clothing lines were also custom-made so much so that the Roman soldiers were "fighting" over them after His crucifixion.

Fashion, music, movies, sports and other forms of entertainment that create an atmosphere of joy, celebration and excitement are not bad in and of themselves. They are amoral tools used to shape a culture. They only become vicious when their intents are not organized pari passu the purpose of God in the earth.

Therefore, if your core gift or ability fits into this mountain of entertainment such as music, sports, acting, or fashion, go for it and let this arena be your platform to establish God's kingdom. This kingdom also has its own sub- categories.

7. THE KINGDOM OF BUSINESS

The ultimate, main goal or desire of people endeavoring to invade this kingdom should be to add value to the human race through service or product or both and then profit in the process. The injunction of Jesus when He said, *"...you are the salt of the earth, ...you are the light of the world... "* (Matthew 5:13) should be their compass.

For the people who don't have covenant with God, their primary objective is to rip people off and maximize their profits. But if God is calling you into this sphere, your main vision is to supply valuable service and product (more on this on the chapter; "Recession is a Myth").

If your core, central gift aligns with business and you believe God will have you function there, then you must be very cautious and develop a systematic, consistent, generous giving spirit. This is so imperative because if you start falling in love with money to a point of greed, you will hurt your soul.

"For the love of money is a root of all kinds of evil, for which some have strayed from the faith in their greediness, and pierced themselves through with many sorrows" (1 Timothy 6:10).

Loving money to a point that you are under its grip and control is a sign that you are under the influence of mammon, the god of money and it is almost impossible to take over a kingdom from the spirit under which you function.

God will usually assign a little to you first and watch how you handle it. If you cannot part with little, you may not grow beyond what you can handle. Although there are many factors responsible for financial abundance apart from generous giving, most of the philosophies discussed in this book will eventually make you wealthy if you are consistent.

An in-depth study of these various kingdoms or spheres of influence will reveal an overwhelming overlap of some of them. They are intrinsically enmeshed in an almost inseparable manner. For example, it's almost impossible to get into politics today without being a professional. There are also some instances where some ministers also own their own television or radio stations.

The key thing is to identify your core, main gift first, develop, and deploy it maximally to a point of significant success. Then you leverage your platform, success and expertise into other areas where you may be equally gifted (More in the chapter; "Leveraging Your Platform and Expertise").

Study Guide

1. There are at least three main synonyms used to describe our responsibilities in shaping the human culture or society. They are spheres, mountains, and kingdoms. Which one is your favorite? Explain three reasons why.
   a.
   b.
   c.

2. Identify the seven kingdoms to take over and explain why in one sentence.
   a.
   b.
   c.
   d.
   e.
   f.
   g.

3. These spheres of influence are closely interrelated. Analyze two or three that you are ready to take over.
   a.
   b.
   c.

4. Discuss your strategy in terms of leverage. In other words, which kingdom do you intend to take over first before leveraging your success into other kingdoms?

5. Do you plan to pursue a higher or professional degree? If yes, is the course relevant to your main gift or calling? If not, you need to reevaluate. Give three reasons why you think that course is relevant.
   a.
   b.
   c.

6. The seven kingdoms have their sub-categories, identify the different sub-categories of three kingdoms you are called into.

    a. Kingdom of .....
       sub-categories   i _____

                                      ii _____

                                      iii _____

                                      iv _____

                                      v _____

    b. Kingdom of ....
       sub-categories   i _____

                                        ii _____

                                      iii _____

                                      iv _____

                                      v _____

    c. Kingdom of .....
       sub-categories   i _____

                                        ii _____

                                      iii _____

                                      iv _____

                                      v _____

7. Write down five spiritual strategies you want to employ to invade these kingdoms.

    a.

    b.

    c.

    d.

    e.

8. Identify three testimonies you have experienced in certain endeavors within the last year as you engaged the spiritual strategies above.

    a.

    b.

    c.

Chapter 21

THE LAST FRONTIER

Understanding The Purpose Of The Message of Grace

As explained earlier, God works in patterns because He loves order. When He allows certain things to happen over and over again then it becomes a pattern.

"By the mouth of two or three witnesses every word shall be established" (2 Corinthians 13:1).

God will never do anything major on the planet without a witness. I believe with so many scriptural evidences and prophetic insights based on the previous patterns and what is happening now that one of the messages that will usher in the greatest move of God on earth is the message of grace. It is one of the last frontier messages.

Grace contextually defined is the unveiling of God's mercy, kindness, compassion, and forgiveness. It is also the revelation and the working of His ability and divine enablement in mortal men. This combination of definitions is what will characterize the last days.

God's pattern has always been a consistent way of carrying out His operation with dispensational variations in methodologies, but the message has always remained the same.

When there was economic recession (famine) in ancient Egypt, God's covenant people were having the best of time in Goshen (a demonstration of God's grace). When the plagues hit, everybody in Egypt except God's covenant people was negatively impacted which prophetically confirms the scenario that Prophet Isaiah described.

"For behold, the darkness shall cover the earth, and deep darkness the people; but the LORD will arise over you, and His glory will be seen upon you" (Isaiah 60:2).

I believe there will be a tremendous outpouring of the revelation (light) and true understanding of grace in these last days. While I do not claim to know everything about grace, no human being does, I am of the opinion that the church of Christ (body of Christ) with all the giant strides she has made has not fully understood it, but she will before Jesus comes.

Because of a parochial understanding of what Jesus Christ and His redemptive works represent, a lot of God's people are still trying to get what they already have, trying to become who they already are and are trying to defeat a defeated foe. All these are obvious in the way we pray and when one skims through our prayer requests. This is because mankind's main problem has always been rooted in identity crisis. Adam and Eve started it all when Satan deceived them,

"For God knows that in the day you eat of it your eyes will be opened, and you will be like God, knowing good and evil" (Genesis 3:5).

But God already created them in His own image and likeness. One of satan's most effective weapons till today is deception. A true revelation of who you are in Christ is available only through the grace of God. When you look unto Jesus, you see who you are. *"Looking unto Jesus, the author and finisher of our faith, who for the joy that was set before Him endured the cross, despising the shame, and has sat down at the right hand of the throne of God"* (Hebrews 12:2).

Grace, which is synonymous with the love of God, does not focus on your sins or weaknesses because whatever you focus on will expand, but focuses on *"Christ in you, the hope of glory"* (Colossians 1:27). The truth is that you can never work enough on your weaknesses otherwise you would never need Jesus. Paul, a once carnal, wicked, serial killer before he encountered grace wrote something powerful and dangerous at the same time. He says, "if you think you can become perfect by your determination and will power outside of Christ, you are insinuating that Jesus' death was in vain" (Galatians 2:21 paraphrased). Paul is implying that the more you focus on yourself and your weaknesses, the less of Jesus you see in the picture and the less of Jesus, the more helpless you become.

True revelation of grace through Christ is not afraid of God but fears Him reverentially. Grace energizes and gives boldness on the premise of Christ's redemption. *"Let us therefore come boldly to the throne of grace, that we may obtain mercy and find grace to help in time of need"* (Hebrews 4:16).

In fact, a man who truly understands God's grace will not sin, not because of its consequences but because he cannot afford to hurt his loving heavenly Father. To him, even if there was no hell, he still won't sin because God says he should not and that settles it.

If your desire to live a holy life is only predicated on the fear of consequences of sin, then your understanding of the Father's love is warped. The question is, what if there were no consequences?

Throughout the pages of the Holy Bible, there are always two ways to attain holiness. One is a lower, more difficult way and the other is a higher and easier way. The lower way of attaining holiness is through dogmas, legalism, observation of laws and religious codes. It is more difficult and a few people are probably doing their best. The motivation for those who have chosen this method is based on the fear of the fire consuming, Almighty God whose judgment can be terrible.

On the other hand, the higher way removes focus on what man can do and focuses on Jesus Christ through His word by developing a son-father or daughter-father relationship with God. The motivation to live holy on this side is not fear, but love. It is grace-based.

Even though God is still seen and honored as the all powerful, fire consuming, majestic God whose judgment can be terrible, the people who have chosen this method know that God is not angry at them and that He is not setting a trap for them to fall so that He can punish them.

A sociological and psychological study of humans reveals that people's perceptions in life are shaped by their environment and belief systems. For instance, a child that is being raised by a high handed, demanding, wicked father may have a challenge accepting God as a loving father. On the other hand, another child being raised by a loving, tender, kind father may not likely struggle with the idea that God is good. And a child that is not being raised by any father at all may even find it difficult to believe in the fatherhood of God. It's all about perception and childhood exposure. That's why Paul encourages the believer to constantly renew his mind in God's word.

"(1)I beseech you therefore, brethren, by the mercies of God, that you present your bodies a living sacrifice, holy, acceptable to God, which is your reasonable service. (2)And do not be conformed to this world, but be transformed by the renewing of your mind, that you may prove what is that good and acceptable and perfect will of God" (Romans 12:1-2).

This higher way of attaining holiness is the last frontier. You may be asking, "are you encouraging licentiousness and careless living?" The answer is an emphatic NO. But I am also saying that there is no sin God cannot forgive except the blasphemy against the Holy Spirit which I believe a truly born again child of God would not commit.

> *The truth is, grace becomes stronger and multiplied where there are too many sins because it is always God's last card to confront sin. Where true grace is understood, the sinner falls at the foot of the cross.*

The truth is, grace becomes stronger and multiplied where there are too many sins because it is always God's last card to confront sin. Where true grace is understood, the sinner falls at the foot of the cross. One of the signs of the last days is the multiplication of sins, *"…lawlessness will abound, the love of many will grow cold"* (Matthew 24:12). However, because of the blood of Jesus Christ and the reality of His redemptive power, grace will also multiply. *"But where sin abounded, grace abounded much more"* (Romans 5:20). You may be asking, "What about Paul's question?" *"What shall we say then? Shall we continue in sin that grace may abound?"* (Romans 6:1). I join Paul to answer "GOD FORBID."

A true believer does not knowingly and willingly live in sin. If he does, even though God will forgive him as many times as he asks for forgiveness, he may go through the consequences of his actions depending on the stipulated applicable laws or repercussions. For instance, if a believer lives in sexual sin consistently, he may risk contracting STDs, destroy his family while living with the shame even though God has forgiven him. He may eventually die an untimely death and go to heaven. If a believer steals consistently, he may be prosecuted and sentenced to jail even though God has forgiven him. He may have to continue his ministry behind the bars. What I am inferring is that the stiff repercussions of these forgivable sins could sometimes be a demonstration of grace.

Certain godly disciplines that may look shameful or embarrassing to leaders especially if they fail to repent after series of secret warnings from the Holy Spirit could be an act of grace as long as the shame will prevent more tragic consequences, hell.

A lot of negative things have been written and said about the last days and we have been made to believe that the only things to look for in the end time prophecies are all negative. Again, what you focus on will expand.

My friend, just like the negatives of eschatology, there are also good things to look for. Marriage is one of them. Jesus alluded to the place of marriage as parts of the events of the last days when he said *"as it was in the days of Noah…when people were giving away their daughters in marriage, so shall it be at the coming of the son of man…"* So what is good about marriage you may ask? God's word says; *"…It is not good that man should be alone; I will make him a helper comparable to him"* (Genesis 2:18). *"Marriage is honorable…"* (Hebrews 13:4).

Covenant marriage is not just about sex and raising children (although they are part of the reasons), it is a typology of the covenant union between Christ and the church. Without that deeper understanding, the individuals in marriage may not fulfill their full potential. Today, as part of Jesus' prophetic allusion, people are getting married every minute across the globe. Whether these marriages are being done properly or not is another subject that would be handled by other people specifically called into this ministry.

Perhaps the greatest, most positive part of eschatology is that of a global outpouring of the Holy Spirit upon everyone.

"(28)And it shall come to pass afterward that I will pour out My Spirit on all flesh; your sons and your daughters shall prophesy, your old men shall dream dreams, your young men shall see visions. (29)And also on My menservants and on My maidservants I will pour out My Spirit in those days" (Joel 2:28-29).

This sounds to me that the individual recipients of this outpouring will not do anything to qualify for it apart from a willing heart. The list of the beneficiaries of this move includes certain people that are below the ladder of social echelon, *"Upon servants and handmaids in those days will I pour out my spirit."*

The power of God orchestrated by grace will fall on people that are regarded as the dregs of the earth, the average people and the have nots, the despised and the peasants. This outpouring will permeate the entire planet in every sphere of human endeavors. I am pretty sure the devil is in a panic mode now because that move is going to devastate him a great deal.

I have always believed that the Holy Spirit will fall on you when you pray, fast, and live a holy life, and that is true to a large extent and this outpouring will have those elements, but more importantly the opposite will also be true. God will pour His grace on those who cannot pray, fast, and are struggling to be holy so they could pray, fast, and live holy. In other words, God will not just anoint us because of what we can do but He will anoint us to do what we cannot do all because of grace through Christ. This happened before: remember how the Holy Spirit interrupted Peter and did not even allow the Gentiles to start "living right" before descending on them? Acts 10:44 says *"While Peter was still speaking these words, the Holy Spirit fell upon all those who heard the word."* When God sends His Spirit, He messes up our theology. As God sends the outpouring of this grace and His love, we will pray like never before, fast, study the word, give like we have never done. We have always done the opposite. We pray, fast, and give so that God can move and there are times for that, but the hour is coming when *"… the goodness of God will lead us to repentance"* (Romans 2:4).

> *I have always believed that the Holy Spirit will fall on you when you pray, fast, and live a holy life, and that is true to a large extent and this outpouring will have those elements, but more importantly the opposite will also be true. God will pour His grace on those who cannot pray, fast, and are struggling to be holy so they could pray, fast, and live holy.*

I believe one of the reasons why God wants to get us out of the way is so that we would not say our prayer, holiness and other efforts were responsible for the outpouring. The apostle Peter rebuked the people who were trying to idolize him and John after healing the crippled man by the beautiful gate. He said, *"…why look so intently at us, as though by our own power or godliness we had made this man walk?"* (Acts 3:12). The implication of his statement is that they were vessels being used by the grace of God. All that would be required of us to do is to enter into His rest as we focus on who Jesus Christ is, and release our faith to be like Him, *"…as He is, so are we in this world"* (1 John 4:17).

The only "labor" will be laboring in the word to get specific revelations in certain areas of our life and the moment we get that "light" (revelation), we enter into His rest in that arena. So I believe there will be an outpouring of outstanding grace for revelation in finance, holiness, family, business, health and other areas where people are struggling now, and each time we labor in the word for specific revelations in those areas and we consistently walk in that light no matter what, we will be at rest.

God's plan has always been that we would serve Him, live holy, without struggling. This can only be done by faith, and through the GRACE OF GOD by focusing on JESUS and His redemptive work. This understanding is highly imperative if we must fulfill and experience our God-given purpose on earth.

Study Guide

---

1. Identify and discuss the synonyms of the word "GRACE."

    _____

    _____

2. There are two main methods to "achieve" holiness. In two sentences each, discuss them.

    1st Method   a. _____

                  b. _____

    2nd Method   a. _____

                  b. _____

3. Identify and discuss five Scriptures on grace with your study group in relation to your core competence.

    a.

    b.

    c.

    d.

    e.

4. Even though the Old Testament saints lived under a limited dispensation, they did many exploits that some believers in a better dispensation today are not doing. If you agree with this statement, write three reasons why this is so and offer solutions to the crisis.

    Reasons   a.

               b.

               c.

    Solution   a.

               b.

               c.

5. List three main areas of your life where you believe you need special grace of God and discuss with your accountability partner or study group for prayer.

6. Discuss Joel 2:28-30 with your colleagues in your study group and create an energetic prayer session afterwards.

Chapter 22

LIFE BEYOND THE GRAVE

Unveiling The Ultimate Purpose

Surrounded with the trappings of flamboyance and a life of fun on a fast lane; girls, cigarettes, alcohol, my life seemed to be slipping away on a particular night. I was watching a late night movie in a friend's house when suddenly I felt a gloomy emptiness in my soul. It was so deep that I became afraid. The presence of my girlfriend, the cigarette within my fingers and the movie I was watching became irrelevant as my whole life lapsed into nothingness.

By the standard of the world of an average man in his early 20s, I wanted to conquer the world. I was the happiest guy. Girls would surround me like bees. Guys wanted me to mentor them on how to date girls and have fun. When I showed up in parties or nightclubs, the shout of "Sparkle Lee" (my nickname before I got saved) would fill the air. I really felt on top of the world.

This particular night was different. A feeling of hollowness and meaninglessness filled my entire being. I was filled with agony. The sad thing was that my girlfriend could not help me. She could not; because she did not understand what was going on. Looking back to that experience in retrospect a few years after my salvation, my conclusion was that God was giving me a clue to eternity without Him. If somebody had told me what to do that night, I would have been born-again on the spot. Of course, I finally ignored that prompting and became "normal" again. Thank God I did not die that night. My soul would have been lost forever. From this experience and other people's I have discovered the following.

1. Everybody is afraid of a life without purpose.
2. Everybody is afraid of the unknown.
3. Everybody is afraid of death.

4. Everybody is afraid of life after death (especially if they are not sure of where they are going).

5. Everybody is in search of a true God including the atheist. His belief system in atheism after a fruitless search without Christ is probably responsible for his conclusion that there is no God. Sadly, most atheists were born by Christian parents but raised in religion instead of a personal, authentic, relationship with Jesus Christ.

6. Nothing on earth can satisfy your longing soul except Christ. Not even sex, alcohol, drugs, cars, money, not even charities as good as they are. That is why this chapter is titled LIFE BEYOND THE GRAVE: Unveiling the Ultimate Purpose.

It is almost impossible to have a meaningful discussion on the subject of purpose without including the reality of eternity. God's ultimate purpose for man does not end in this physical realm. The most important purpose of all time begins on the other side of this life. Discussions on life after death have been taken to the platforms of psychology and spirituality. Some question the reality of heaven or hell. To some people, eternity is a myth, it does not exist and some believe it exists with various approaches to its interpretation. Most of the people who don't believe in the immortality of the soul hinge their belief system on the atheistic philosophy of lack of belief in the existence of God. Some believe that man lives forever, but goes through a purgatorial journey after death after which his soul will finally rest forever.

> *God's ultimate purpose for man does not end in this physical realm. The most important purpose of all time begins on the other side of this life.*

These different belief systems have formed the basis for certain philosophical schools of thought that are shaping the way people think today. For instance, the Epicureans or the Hedonists believe that life should be enjoyed maximally before one dies putting their premise on sensuality. The only problem with that is, to them, life must be lived to its best independent of God because man is capable of governing himself. This philosophy is rationally based on humanism, that is, man is his own god. Their belief is like the ideas of certain Epicureans, which Paul encountered in the Acts of the Apostles (Acts 17:18).

Stoics on the other hand live on the philosophy of doing the right thing every time regardless of one's emotional impulse because it is what guarantees a life of self-discipline and virtue. Most ancient writers, including the foremost English playwright, William Shakespeare expanded this theory in *King Lear*. The king who is ignorant of the daughter who loves him most among his three daughters is deceived and suffers untold hardship. So he moves from ignorance to suffering and from suffering into discipline and wisdom. The only problem with this philosophy is, it falls short of what Christ came to do: All these philosophies and schools of thoughts are primarily based on rational intellectualism without Christ.

"For this purpose the Son of God was manifested, that He might destroy the works of the devil" (1 John 3:18).

You see, an attempt is being made by satan to distort the truth by mixing elements of truth with lie to spread heresy. While there could be a season in your life when you endure pain (Stoicism), there is also a time to "spoil" and "enjoy" your life (Epicureanism). However, the balance is, whether you are enduring pain for a moment or having a blast, your experience must be seen through the lens of God's impeccable word and that should be your final authority.

The truth is, because God is so generous, He has given every human being the freedom of choice with the right to choose what they believe and where they want to go at the end of this life. But because He wants the best for you, He is always trying to get your attention through His word, nature, conscience, and circumstances to make you choose wisely. In spite of the various evidences about the reality of hell and heaven, countless individuals still make the choice to ignore Christ and slip into eternity without God daily. The Bible gives a graphic, vivid account of hell as a place of eternal torment, agony, horror, and a place of no return; a place of indescribable, unquenchable thirst and a place of damnable depression. The most horrible part of hell may not even be the inferno itself, as horrible as that would be, but there is nothing more horrifying as the absence of the presence of God. Hell is a hopeless place.

HELL IS WHERE POSSESSION DOES NOT MATTER

"For what will it profit a man if he gains the whole world, and loses his own soul?" (Mark 8:36).

Read these last words of a few dying atheists.

HELL IS A PLACE OF LONELINESS AND DEPRESSION
"Until this moment I thought there was neither a God nor a hell. Now I know and feel that they are both and I am doomed to perdition by the just judgment of the Almighty." -Sir Thomas Scott

HELL IS A PLACE WHERE IT IS ALWAYS TOO LATE TO MAKE IT RIGHT
Talking to Dr. Fochin, "I am abandoned by God and man, I will give you half of what I'm worth if you will give me six months' life." "It could not be done" responded the doctor. "Then I shall die and go to hell." -Voltaire

HELL IS A PLACE OF AGONY AND ETERNAL REGRET
"I am lost, lost, lost. I am damned, damned, damned forever." His agony was so terrible that he tore his hair as he passed into eternity. -An unknown infidel

HELL IS AD INFINITUM
"Oh the insufferable pangs of hell, eternity forever and ever." -Sir Frances Newport

HELL IS A PLACE OF INTELLECTUAL PAROCHIALISM
"What a fool I have been." -Charles Churchill

Perhaps the most horrific part of hell is: it is a place where the person who chooses to go is BEYOND REDEMPTION.

"Demons are in my room ready to drag my soul down to hell. It is no use looking to Jesus now: it is too late." -Brown

The purpose of these last words by people who faced the reality of hell is not to intimidate or scare you but to let you see the danger of taking a risk by not believing and making Jesus Christ your Savior, so that like Brown, it will not be too late. The good news is that you can receive Christ into your life this minute by simply confessing your sins to Him and inviting Him into your life as your Savior and you'll be saved right away. Originally, hell was not created for any human being but for the devil and his angels and those who reject the redemptive work of Jesus Christ on the cross.

Just like we have agonizing, heart wrenching last words of sinners, there are also the last words of a few dying saints. Heaven is a place of eternal bliss, joy and peace. But more importantly, a place where God lives. His presence alone is worth more than all the glamour in heaven and earth put together. His presence is everything. That is the eternal home of every one that has been redeemed by the blood of Jesus and who accepted Him in their hearts as Savior. No wonder the Bible says;

"…Let me die the death of the righteous, and let my end be like his" (Numbers 23:10).

Apostle Paul died the death of the righteous;

"(6)For I am already being poured out as a drink offering, and the time of my departure is at hand. (7)I have fought the good fight, I have finished the race, I have kept the faith. (8)Finally, there is laid up for m the crown of righteousness, which the Lord, the righteous Judge, will give to me on that Day, and not to me only but also to all who have loved His appearing" (2 Timothy 4:6-8). Stephen also died the same way;

"(57)Then they cried out with a loud voice, stopped their ears, and ran at him with one accord; (58)and they cast him out of the city and stoned him. And the witnesses laid down their clothes at the feet of a young man named Saul. (59)And they stoned Stephen as he was calling on God and saying, "Lord Jesus, receive my spirit." (60)Then he knelt down and cried out with a loud voice, "Lord, do not charge them with this sin." And when he had said this, he fell asleep" (Acts 7:57-60).

HEAVEN IS A PLACE OF ETERNAL REST
"Lord Jesus, I am weary in thy work, but not of thy work. I have not yet finished my course, let me go and speak for thee once more in the field, seal the truth and come home to die."-George Whitefield

HEAVEN IS A PLACE OF BEAUTY AND SERENITY
"I know I am dying, but my death bed is a bed of roses. I have no thorns planted upon my dying pillow. Heaven has already begun."
-John Pawson

HEAVEN IS A PLACE OF PEACE AND ETERNAL GLORY
"Earth recedes. Heaven opens before me. If this is death, it is sweet. There is no valley here. God is calling me and I must go ... This is my triumph; this is my coronation day. It is glorious."-Dwight L. Moody

ETERNITY AND ACADEMICS

This discussion on eternity and life after death may not have an acceptable basis for intellectual argument because it cannot be proven by empirical studies except through death, the ultimate Grim Reaper. So, I am not proffering a theory of catharsis by writing about heaven. However, what I do know is that there are intellectual justifications and historical facts about the ONE that can prevent you from going to hell and take you to heaven. His name is Jesus Christ.

> *This discussion on eternity and life after death may not have an acceptable basis for intellectual argument because it cannot be proven by empirical studies except through death, the ultimate Grim Reaper.*

Throughout human history, honest people of all ages from different persuasions, philosophies or religions have affirmed that Jesus Christ of Nazareth is the most outstanding personality of all times. There is no history without Him. Historical facts are mangled or distorted without the person of Jesus Christ of Nazareth. He has changed the entire landscape of history. "Even dates are calculated before and after Him. B.C. means 'Before Christ' and A.D. *Anno Domini*, a Latin word translated 'in the year of the Lord'" writes Bill Bright of Campus Crusade.

I personally firmly believe that the historical facts and truth of His birth, nativity, and earthly ministry are all evidenced in the Bible by real, authentic, Holy Spirit inspired writers who wrote at different times and locations but have an unusual synergy in their presentations of fundamental truths that are devoid of any literary cacophony.

Even more modern contemporary scholars attest to this unity. Dr. Clifford Herbert Moore, former professor at Harvard University writes:

"Christianity knows its Savior and Redeemer, not as some god whose history was contained in a mythical faith, with rude, primitive and even offensive elements. The Christian faith is founded on positive, historical and acceptable facts."

I absolutely agree with Moore's proposition when one looks at the giant strides countries in the west have made because of their acceptance of Christ's values and the decline they are now experiencing as they allow those values to erode. Christianity brings civilization and freedom.

Still on historical facts of Jesus and the positive influence of His teachings, William Lyon Phelps, a professor at Yale University for four years and a professing believer who confidently shares his faith also intelligently attests to the human-lifting values in Christ doctrines. A professor at Oxford University, C.S. Lewis who was for years a skeptic and agnostic finally came to the foot of the cross when convicted after a series of researches in the Bible and other historical facts about the Savior of the world.

In *Mere Christianity*, he writes, "...that is why the Christian is in a different position from other people who are trying to be good...the Christian thinks any good he does comes from the Christ-life inside him..." In other words, Jesus' sacrificial death on the cross and our acceptance of it is what guarantees our freedom and not our efforts. Even the historical resurrection facts and truth are further corroborated by John Singleton Copley, a famous and highly respected British lawyer and historian. "I know pretty well what evidence is and I tell you, such as that for the resurrection has never broken down yet and never will."

CONCLUSION

As you must have read from the previous chapters, the main thesis of this book has been to show the vast investments God has put in man. Identifying them, developing, and deploying them by taking advantage of all the strategies discussed will almost automatically create a suitable platform for the fulfillment of God's purpose for your life.

Also, you will notice that my emphasis so far has not just been on purpose, but on the creation of platforms to fulfilling it.

Let me conclude by postulating from the Bible that it is possible to fulfill certain elements of one's purpose in life by focusing on the gifts without actually knowing God. Reason being that some of the principles for doing that are universal ones that would work for anybody regardless of his belief system, age, race, religion or gender.

The danger however is equating adding values to human beings with doing the will of God and as such that should automatically take you to heaven. People don't go to heaven because of good works but because they have a personal relationship with God through Jesus Christ and are born-again Christians, but born-again Christians should do good works.

THE SEVEN CLASSES OF PEOPLE ON EARTH

It is my strong belief through extensive, recent researches and God's word that there are seven main classes of people on the planet. There could be more sub-groups under these.

(1) **Purpose-fulfilling non-Christians:** Those that will identify certain elements of their God-given gifts, develop and deploy their core gifts to create a platform for the fulfillment of their God-given purpose but don't have a relationship with Christ. They will have relative enjoyment, happiness and success in this world but will go to hell in the last day.

(2) **Purpose-ignoring Christians:** Those that have a relationship with Christ but are so much heaven conscious that they are not interested in contributing anything to humanity. They have no idea of their core gift let alone develop or deploy it. They will relatively suffer on earth especially in the area of finance, but they will make heaven in the last day (Ex. Lazarus in Luke 16:19-31).

(3) **Purpose-ignoring non-Christians:** Those that are neither number 1 or 2. They don't have any relationship with Christ and they are not interested in any gift or creating any platform to help anybody. They will have the worst of the two worlds. They will suffer untold hardship here on earth and still go to hell on the last day (Ex. Judas Iscariot).

(4) **Purpose-searching Christians:** Those that have a healthy relation- ship with Jesus Christ and are in the process of discovering their core gift with which to create a platform from where they will fulfill their purpose. They could enjoy this world relatively if they successfully create their platform and will also make heaven.

(5) **Purpose-wasting people:** Those that would identify, develop, and deploy their core gifts to create platform but would NOT fulfill their purpose. They are the influential people who later make poor choices and are now living wasted lives behind prison bars.

If they are not saved, they will go to hell (Ex. Judas Iscariot).

(6) Purpose-delaying people: Those that have identified their purpose and the core gift with which to pursue it but have the following attitudes towards it.

    a. Apathy: People who are indifferent towards their purpose in life.

    b. Laziness: Those who do not want to do anything about their gift and purpose.

    c. Procrastination: Those who are always putting off what they can do about their gift and purpose.

This category of people will not make any significant impact in this world and where they spend their eternity depends on their choice, God or Satan.

(7) Purpose-fulfilling Christians: The final group is the most interesting. They are those who have a personal relationship with Christ and have identified their core gifts, and are constantly developing and deploying them. They will enjoy the best of the two worlds. They will have a blast here on earth (success, abundance, peace, joy etc) and will make heaven their ete home. Joseph, David, the patriarchs, and all the saints ar this category. I pray you'll be in this group.

It is my hope that this book has answered some of the questions associated with your God-given purpose and the practicality of its fulfillment. It is my prayer that your energy is being triggered and galvanized in the direction of making wise choices that will help you create a sustainable, life-changing system that leads to a meaningful life in this world and an eternal bliss with God through our Savior and Lord, Jesus Christ. It is also my heart-felt desire to meet you in person one of these days, but if it doesn't happen, let's stay connected in the spirit.

Love you.

Study Guide

1. Life after death cannot be a subject of empirical study: Discuss with your group.

2. Discuss three philosophies of intellectual catharsis that have no redemptive values.
   a.
   b.
   c.

3. What is your understanding of the immortality of the soul? Discuss.

4. Identify one of the scholastic arguments in favor of Jesus Christ and discuss the indispensable reality of His saving Grace.

5. Write down the seven classes of people on earth in relation to gift and purpose and explain three of them with real life examples.
   a.
   b.
   c.
   d.
   e.
   f.
   g.

   Explain three of them here.
   a.
   b.
   c.

Synopsis

Chapter 1: THE ANATOMY OF PURPOSE
The Four Pillars of Purpose

There are four main elements of any God-given purpose.

They are also called pillars. These are the foundations on which everybody's purpose should rest. They are:

    a.   The universality of purpose

    b.   The immutability of purpose

    c.   The profitability of purpose

    d.   Glorifying the source of purpose

Chapter 2: GIFT VERSUS PURPOSE
The Dichotomy I

This chapter focuses on the main, fundamental differences between gift and purpose. It is possible for a man to be gifted and not fulfill purpose. It also examines the difference between the Adamic, pre-existence gift and ascension gift and how both are necessary for the fulfillment of one's destiny.

Chapter 3: PASSION VERSUS PURPOSE
The Dichotomy II

Passion is not exactly the same thing as purpose. It is possible for a man to be passionate about what is completely irrelevant to his purpose in life. Your passion only becomes relevant when it lines up with your dominant gift and purpose.

Chapter 4: FOUR STAGES OF COMPETENCE
Your Life Assignment versus Your Career

Behavioral scientists and psychologists came up with the concept of stages of the human developments.

The scriptural equivalent of the theory is also underscored in this chapter. The stages are:

    a.   Unconscious Incompetence

    b.   Conscious Incompetence

    c.   Conscious Competence

    d.   Unconscious Competence

The basic difference between a work and a job is also examined.

Chapter 5: MULTIPLE INTELLIGENCES AND MULTI-GIFTEDNESS—Information Overload Debunked

While it is imperative to gather important, adequate information before crucial decisions are taken, irrelevant information in an age of information overload has become the bane of the 21st century. The theory of multiple intelligences and the need to be laser focused on one's core competence is extensively discussed.

Chapter 6: THE EAGLE'S EYE
Making the Main Thing, the Main Thing

For anyone to succeed and make progress in any life's endeavor, there has to be a mindset called Intensity of Focus. Without it, the individual may crumble in the midst of many distractions. This chapter addresses issues relating to multiple gifts and abilities.

Chapter 7: THE POWER OF SIMPLICITY
Uncluttering your Core Gift

Identifying the core gift with which to fulfill purpose is probably one of the major challenges confronting many people today. There are eight questions that address this issue in a very, relatable, practical way. These questions are universal. Giving honest, objective answers to them will leave anybody with a feeling of absolute clarity of their gifts and destiny.

Chapter 8: PRO-ACTIVE TARGET PRACTICE
Putting Pressure on Your Core Intelligence

Knowing one's core gift with which to pursue purpose is not enough, developing it through constant, target practice is imperative for its deployment. There has to be a deliberate, intentional, pro-active exercise of this gift until the use of it becomes second nature.

Chapter 9: SYSTEMATIC TRANSITION STRATEGIES
Before You Fire Your Boss

Success and progress in life must have a strategic plan. The Bible is filled with successful people who planned strategically. It is not just enough to know the core gift you will use to fulfill your purpose, there must be a systematic transition in place. There are over thirteen practical tips to study before you fire your boss.

Chapter 10: SEARCHING FOR A NEEDLE IN A HAYSTACK
Creative Branding System for Effective Transition

Our world is becoming more increasingly competitive through aggressive globalization. It is not business as usual. It is possible to be misunderstood if perception is wrong. The need to brand and stand out is not only necessary, it is urgently needed. This chapter focuses on personal branding, the importance of branding and the consequences of ignoring it.

Chapter 11: RECESSION IS A MYTH
The Wealthy Poor

Recession, which has become a dreadful word in today's world of global, economic uncertainty, has finally been demystified. The code has been cracked. What people call recession is actually supposed to put pressure on people's gifts, abilities and creativities. It is a perfect storm for creative, value-adding covenant people. No cent has left the planet, money is just moving around. It's a liquid; it simply flows into the direction of those who understand its philosophy. This chapter underscores how.

Chapter 12: RELATIONSHIP EQUITY
Building a Sustainable Platform

Everything you will ever do to fulfill your God-given purpose and the resources to do it is tied to other human beings. No one is sent to spirits or angels. The understanding of this truth is necessary so that other human beings created in the image of God are treated with respect. Sensitive and complex issues that threaten the effectiveness of God's gifts and purpose in relation to how people mortgage their purpose because of poor management of strategic relationships are practically discussed.

Chapter 13: THE THEORY OF REVERSE NEGATIVES
Creating Energy for Your Core Gift and Purpose

The journey to the fulfillment of purpose is already fraught with challenges that are capable of draining one's energy. No one needs extra, self-inflicted punishment added to the complexities of the journey. The devil uses negative emotions all the times to weigh people down through guilt, condemnation and self-pity. This chapter discusses how the theory of reverse negatives can be applied to maintain balance between extremes. A good understanding of this law will reveal that people are not as bad as they think.

Chapter 14: LOOKING FOR THE LIVING IN THE MIDST OF THE DEAD—Creative Marketing System

There is a general, naïve notion that because the product or the service is good, it will sell itself. While that is true to some extent, the caveat is, products or services only sell when people are aware they exist. Creative marketing and systematic publicity campaign for valuable product or services should never be taken for granted. This chapter focuses on the power of marketing. Before, it was all about who you knew. Now, it is about who knows you.

Chapter 15: MARKETING IS SPIRITUAL
Overcoming Shame Associated with Marketing

Most people don't want to accept they are marketers and that they are in sales because of the stigma associated with selling. The truth is, everybody is selling something. When people recommend a nice movie or restaurant to their friends or family members, it is called marketing or sales. Jesus trained twelve disciples to go and "sell" His vision to everybody who cared to listen. He also said that our "light," which in this context could be product or service, should not be hidden. The chapter unveils acceptable, decent, scriptural reasons why people should not be ashamed to advertise their values.

Chapter 16: LEVERAGING YOUR EXPERTISE, PLATFORM, AND SUCCESS—Giants Living In The Shadow

Leveraging is a powerful word that has been relegated to the background because of ignorance. This chapter critically examines how success in your core competence should not remain on the shelf but should be leveraged into other areas where you are equally gifted.

The components of a systematic leveraging include

1. Your Platform
2. Your Experience
3. Your Integrity
4. Your Brand
5. Your expertise

Chapter 17: WEALTH TRANSFER DEMYSTIFIED
Understanding God's Consistent Patterns

Many have thought that the imminent, prophetic wealth transfer will be completely spiritual in nature. While this is true to a large extent, the real-life, intelligent access method through God's wisdom is scripturally examined, drawing parallels from historical antecedents.

Chapter 18: GETTING THE HORSE READY
The Power Factor

One of the challenges of our world is inability to maintain a reasonable balance between extremes. While there is a need to get involved in your own rescue by bringing your gift and values to the table, it must also be understood that God's power is inevitable in the journey to purpose.

The anointing of God and how to trigger it in the direction of your core gift with which to fulfill your destiny is pragmatically examined in this chapter.

Chapter 19: ENGAGING YOUR ASSETS
Laying Down Your Gift at the Feet of the Giver

Everything we all will ever need to live a meaningful and productive life of purpose has been given to us by God. It is our responsibility to identify those resources after which we lay them down at His feet for purification.

It seems it is a consistent pattern with God to always ask people to give Him back what He has given them so that they can be multiplied.

Chapter 20: KINGDOMS TAKEOVER
The Dominion Mandate

God's plan for the earth has never changed. He wants it to become the colony of heaven through His children when they exercise their dominion mandate.

The kingdom of God and its influence on every sphere of human endeavor, and the dethronement of demonic cartels and mafias is the main focus of this chapter. The culture of heaven must permeate every landscape as we superimpose the reign of Christ on the seven kingdoms.

Chapter 21: THE LAST FRONTIER
Understanding the Purpose of The Message of Grace

Grace, one of the most misunderstood words in Christianity is didactically examined in the context of the last days' move of God.

The two-fold definition of grace and its nature is vividly and lucidly analyzed.

Our understanding of grace goes to another level when we focus on God's love for us rather than on our love for Him.

Chapter 22: LIFE BEYOND THE GRAVE
Unveiling The Ultimate Purpose

The subject of the immortality of the soul is the main theme in this chapter. There is life beyond the grave. The soul of man lives forever and he has a choice of where he wants to live for eternity: Heaven or Hell. This chapter also examines the last words of certain, real, dying men without Christ and those who died in Christ. The chapter paints a vivid, undeniable picture of the reality of the two places.

It concludes with the seven categories of people currently living on earth.

TEN RECOMMENDED ACTION STEPS

1. Get a note pad and a pen. Write down your core gifts, your other gifts and everything you will love to accomplish. Don't be intimidated by the volume. Write everything.

2. Start prioritizing them in their order of importance as far as your purpose is concerned.

3. Identify the core gift that you believe will help you achieve those priorities.

4. Write down your plans for leveraging into the other goals you have written down in (1) above.

5. Examine your values and character. Do you think your present level of character is strong enough to sustain the volume of your vision? If no, write down five strategies you will employ to address the issue.

    i. _____

    ii. _____

    iii. _____

    iv. _____

    v. _____

6. Endeavor to read the book again after three months by paying particular attention to the notes you've taken.

7. Discuss or go through the study guides with a group on a weekly basis. If you don't have a study group, start one.

8. If the book has truly blessed you, please recommend it to everyone in your circle of influence (family members, pastor, friends, neighbors, classmates, your local book stores, libraries etc). If your loved ones cannot afford it, you could pay it forward by buying the book for them. You'll always get a discount for bulk orders). Our collective purpose is to help as many people as possible.

9. Let us connect through any of the following mediums: Facebook, website, Twitter, email, etc. I want to hear your comments and testimonies. See the contact information on the other page.

10. Achieving God's purpose through your dominant gift is great and fulfilling but the ultimate purpose is an eternal bliss with God. Are you sure you are sincerely saved? If yes, congrats. If no, take

the ultimate action now. Confess your sins to God and invite Jesus Christ into your life as your Savior and Lord. Then get into a Bible-based church and you are guaranteed to have the best of two worlds: Heaven on Earth and a life of absolute, eternal peace with God.

About The Author

Sam Ore is a multi-gifted, charismatic communicator and a conference speaker. By God's grace, he has been involved in many successful enterprises including co-founding a multi-million dollar business in the Washington, DC metro area from scratch. He was also a top notch marketing executive for two Fortune 500 corporations for a few years before resigning to focus on his core intelligence which is communicating the gospel in a practical, twenty-first century context.

He and his wife, Debby are the founders and Senior pastors of Kingdom Ambassadors Christian Center, a multi-racial, multi-national, vibrant Church presently located in Largo, Maryland from where they are raising and empowering influential Godly leaders through the demonstration of the power of God and the word of faith.

Sam Ore's passionate, consuming vision in life is to help other people achieve theirs. There are factual, eloquent testimonies to this truth in the lives of his protégés who are experiencing their purpose in various countries across the globe. They include successful, Godly pastors, business people, politicians, bankers, lawyers, doctors and other professionals.

He and his beautiful wife live with their four Godly children in Silver Spring, Maryland.

Contact Information

Sam Ore
Kingdom Ambassadors Christian Center
9475 Lottsford Road, Suite 110
Largo
Maryland 20774
USA

Phone: 301-494-5400
Email: **pastor@kacconline.org**
Website: **www.samoreglobalempowerment.com**

Please include your testimony of help received from this book when you write. Your prayer requests are also welcome.

You can order additional copies of this book or any other book by the author online @

www.amazon.com
www.barnesandnoble.com
www.kacconline.org

or simply send an email to the above address or place a call to the phone number.

Other Books By The Author

EMPOWERED
(Living Life Beyond Limitations)

Are you tired of living below your potential, held down by limiting circumstances and forces? Do you desire to have God's power at work in your life from day to day in all that you do? Do you want success and elevation in your career or ministry and freedom for your family?

In this powerful book, Sam Ore, using his characteristic easy-to-understand approach, shows how you can be empowered to live the winning life, rising above the limitations you face in the actualization of your destiny in life. He shows clearly and with authority that the ability to excel, win, prosper and live victoriously is available to you right now in the anointing of the Holy Spirit.

You will discover:

- What it means to be empowered
- How to walk in the anointing on purpose, maintaining a fresh flow everyday
- How to position yourself for the release of God's power to change seemingly impossible situations, and much more
- Get ready to make the power of God a prominent and active part of your everyday living through EMPOWERED!

TOWARDS A PURPOSEFUL MARRIAGE
(A Practical Guide for Singles)

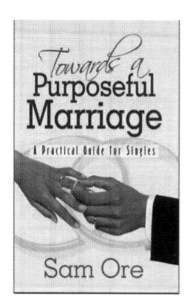

The marriage institution is under the severest attack these days. Statistics reveal an alarming rate of divorce, separation and unhappy unions.

In this book, Sam Ore, using his characteristic simple and practical approach, biblically sheds light on the steps you should take as a single person to lay a proper foundation for your marriage, hence overcoming marriage's toughest challenges even before the wedding day. This book is a must-read for all singles, married, newly weds, marriage counselors, pastors, and parents.

You will discover how to:

- Find the will of God in marriage
- Unleash the favor that marriage brings
- Diagnose and correct the symptoms of an unhealthy relationship
- Manage conflicts in relationships and apply the power factors for bliss in marriage, and much more.

Bibliography

1. Adams, Herbert. COLUMBUS AND HIS DISCOVERY OF AMERICA, John Hopkins Press, 1892.

2. Adelaja, Sunday. CHURCH SHIFT, Charisma House, 2008.

3. Akinmola, Bankole. UNDERSTANDING GOD'S PURPOSE FOR MARRIAGE, Discipling the Harvest Publishing, 2008.

4. Armstrong, Thomas. 7 KINDS OF SMART: Identifying and developing your multiple intelligences, Plume (Penguin-Putnam).

5. Chapman, Gary. THE MARRIAGE YOU HAVE ALWAYS WANTED, Moody Publishers, 2005.

6. Dollar, Creflo A. 8 STEPS TO CREATE THE LIFE YOU WANT: The Anatomy of A Successful Life, Faith words, 2008.

7. Enlow, Johnny. THE SEVEN MOUNTAIN PROPHECY, Creation House, 2008.

8. Gardner, Howard. FRAMES OF MIND: The Theory of multiple intelligences, New York: Basic Books 1983, 1993.

9. Goodwin, Doris Kearns. TEAM OF RIVALS: The Political Genius of Abraham Lincoln, Simeon & Schuster, 2005.

10. Graham, Billy. STORM WARNING: Whether Global Recession, Terrorists threats or devastating natural disasters, these ominous shadows must bring us back to the gospel, Thomas Nelson, 2010.

11. John, Daymond. THE BRAND WITHIN: The power of Branding from birth to the Boardroom, Display of Power Publishing, 2010.

12. Kremer, John. 1001 WAYS TO MARKET YOUR BOOK, Open Horizon, 2011.

13. Lewis, C.S. MERE CHRISTIANITY, www.wikipedia.org/wiki/mere_christianity.

14. McNeal III, Delatorro. CAUGHT BETWEEN A DREAM AND A JOB: How to leave the 9-to-5 Behind and Step into the life you've always wanted, Excel Books, 2008.

15. Meyer, Joyce A LEADER IN THE MAKING: Essentials To Being A Leader After God's own Heart, Warner Faith, 2001.

16. Munroe, Myles. REDISCOVERING THE KINGDOM, Destiny Image, 2004.

17. Munroe, Myles. THE PRINCIPLES AND BENEFITS OF CHANGE, Whitaker House, 2009.

18. Munroe, Myles. THE PURPOSE AND POWER OF AUTHORITY: Discovering the power of your personal Domain, Whitaker, 2011.

19. Ore, Sam. EMPOWERED: Living life Without Limitations, Summit House publishers, 2005.

20. Ore, Sam. TOWARDS A PURPOSEFUL MARRIAGE: A Practical Guide for Singles, Summit House Publishers, 2005.

21. Otabil, Mensa. PATHWAYS OF SUCCESS: 21 Steps on the way to the Top, Blaze Publishing, 2008.

22. Ramsey, Dave. FINANCIAL PEACE, Viking, 2003.

23. Scwawbel, Dan. ME 2.0, Kaplan Publishing, 2009.

24. Silbiger, Steven. THE JEWISH PHENOMENON: Seven Keys to the Enduring Wealth of A People, Long Street Press, 2000.

25. SUCCESS MAGAZINE: Success Media, October 2009 – February 2011.

26. Trump, Donald. THINK LIKE A BILLIONAIRE: Everything You need to know about Success, Real Estate and life, Random House, 2004.

27. Weber, Steve. PLUG YOUR BOOK, Online Book Marketing for authors, WEBER Books, 2007.

93665799R00133

Made in the USA
Columbia, SC
18 April 2018